"John Perkins, you are like fine wine. Y age."

Jim Wallis, pre
best.

"I've known John Perkins for forty years. He is an icon in racial reconciliation and community development. More personally, John has had a lasting impact on me, helping to shine a healing light on my own latent racism. At a time when the racial divide in the United States is widening into a chasm, I cannot think of a more needed message than this book."

Philip Yancey, bestselling Christian author/speaker

"John Perkins is the father of the Christian reconciliation movement. He paved the way for those of us who have become leaders of reconciliation from a Christian perspective. His mantle of leadership is being passed on to those who follow him. Few people have demonstrated longevity and integrity in this work. John Perkins is one of those people, and I am honored to call him my father in the work of reconciliation. I highly recommend this book."

Dr. Brenda Salter McNeil, author of *Roadmap to Reconciliation*

"The light from within Dr. John Perkins shines so brightly that you can't help but be impacted and changed once you've met him and listened to him share stories from his life. The love of Jesus that emanates from him is so real and true; it's living proof that he has won battles in his own life, overcoming incredible hate with supernatural love. He gives us all hope to believe that love really is the final fight that we can win. I am grateful for his life, leadership, and courage to share his story with us yet again, leaving his legacy of love for generations to come."

Judah Smith, lead pastor of The City Church;
New York Times bestselling author of *Jesus Is _____*

"When historians look back at the story of the evangelical church in the United States, one of the shining lights will be the life and impact of Dr. John Perkins. Dr. Perkins's role in how American Christians returned to the biblical value of justice in the twentieth century cannot be overstated. This book reveals a critical narrative that must be engaged by those who seek the very best that American evangelicalism can be. To read the inside story and discover the profound move of God in Dr. Perkins's life and ministry is a gift you do not want to miss."

Soong-Chan Rah, Milton B. Engebretson professor of church growth and evangelism, North Park Theological Seminary; author of *The Next Evangelicalism* and *Return to Justice*

"John Perkins's new book, *Dream with Me*, is wonderful. Through John's dreams throughout his life, fantastic things have happened in our world. This book encourages me to dream big, and I highly recommend it for everyone. I love John, and I love his book!"

Reverend Dr. Wayne "Coach" Gordon, founding pastor of Lawndale Christian Community Church; president emeritus of the board of directors, Christian Community Development Association

"I lost my last grandfather in 1995, and since then I've had the honor of having Dr. Perkins (or 'Pops,' as I like to call him) as my adopted grandfather. Whatever credit I've received or good I've done in the area of race relations was inspired by Pops. I've merely followed the long, loving, arduous yet Christ-exalting trail he has blazed—a trail I plan to continue trekking until God calls me home. As I journey onward, I will carry his vulnerable and heart-stirring book, *Dream with Me*, and return to it time and time again for inspiration and sustenance in the days ahead."

Bryan Loritts, lead pastor of Abundant Life Christian Fellowship; author of *Saving the Saved*

"Prophet, legend, lover of humanity—these are words that accurately describe John Perkins. His inspiring example, penetrating writing, and convicting oratory have shaped the history of his time. *Dream with Me* captures in living color personal details of his legacy. A treasure."

Bob Lupton, community developer and author

"*Dream with Me* is an incredible peek into the life and motivation of a civil rights legend and lover of Jesus. This book has the feel of sitting on the front porch with your granddaddy. In these pages, John Perkins reveals the secret ingredient to his life's work and to justice in America—love. An absolute must-read!"

Albert Tate, pastor of Fellowship Monrovia

"Dr. John Perkins is a living legend! He's been a mentor, friend, and role model in my life for more than forty years. While there is today an ever-increasing chorus of people committed to racial reconciliation and justice, John Perkins was one among the few who spoke clearly and prophetically during a dark, challenging time. He literally laid his life on the line for the sake of truth, love, justice, and reconciliation. Thanks, John, for giving me and so many others the courage to press on. Although we may give recognition to people for their accomplishments, we honor them for what they have sacrificed. I love and honor you, my dear friend and mentor."

Dr. Crawford W. Loritts Jr., author; speaker; radio host; senior pastor of Fellowship Bible Church

"There's much to admire about Dr. John Perkins. We could list his talks, books, and accolades, but when I think about Dr. Perkins's leadership and legacy, I'm reminded that a life faithfully lived through hardships, trials, and messiness is one's greatest contribution. This is why I so appreciate his latest book, *Dream with Me*. His posture is not one of arrogance or accomplishment but, rather, of astonishment—at what God has done and what God can do in and among us. And in a world of so much pain, fear, and division, we need to desperately be reminded of God's reconciling truth, grace, and love."

Rev. Eugene Cho, pastor and humanitarian; author of *Overrated*

"Dr. Perkins is such a potent voice to a world in so much need. *Dream with Me* lays out the truth of living the full gospel, of counting the cost of loving whom Jesus loves and how Jesus loves. If anyone who calls Jesus Lord is remotely considering doing the work He's called us to, of doing justice, and living a life of reconciliation, then this is a must-read. What a beautiful blend of hard truth rooted in faith, hope, and love. Dr. Perkins has dedicated his life to this kind of sacrificial love and has remained unhardened. This book calls out the sin that divides us, while simultaneously pointing to the power of the Savior who has already paid the price to unite us. *Dream with Me* brings it all within reach."

Michael Patz, lead pastor of Greenhouse Church

"For over a half century, John Perkins has led the call for people of faith to recognize that God requires justice for the poor and oppressed. Dr. Perkins is one of this nation's most powerful, persistent, and persuasive voices on how faith dies when it is blind to injustice, poverty, and suffering. This beautiful book is a great gift from a legendary, national treasure. I first heard John Perkins preach when I was a teenager in college over thirty years ago. His words stirred me in ways I can still recall. *Dream with Me* makes it clear that Dr. Perkins still has much to say to stir the soul."

Bryan Stevenson, executive director of Equal Justice Initiative

"Thirty-five years ago, I met John Perkins through the late Tom Skinner, his soul brother in ministry for an America that reflects God's redeeming, reconciling love for all people. That dream, told powerfully through John's amazing life's journey and ministry of help, healing, and hope, offers an authentic framework for addressing the systemic racism of our time. *Dream with Me* is a must-read for people of all races and backgrounds who are dreaming and working toward an America united through every tribe, language, people, and nation!"

Dr. Barbara Williams-Skinner, president of
Skinner Leadership Institute

"In an age of painful polarization and divisive rhetoric, no other person in the United States today is more familiar with struggle, more intimate with forgiveness, or more credible to speak of love without distinctions than Dr. John M. Perkins. His invitation is not only to dream with him but, more significantly, to live as he lives and love as he loves. His experiential knowledge, thoughtful reflection, and tested wisdom are prophetic in nature and apostolic in tone. Dr. Perkins is a peacemaker. We would do well to listen to his words, hear his heart, and join him on the ancient path."

Dr. Mark DeYmaz, founding pastor of Mosaic Church
of Central Arkansas; president of Mosaix Global Network;
author of *Disruption* and *Building a Healthy Multiethnic Church*

DREAM WITH ME

DREAM WITH ME

*Race, Love, and the Struggle
We Must Win*

—ʍ—

JOHN M. PERKINS

BakerBooks
a division of Baker Publishing Group
Grand Rapids, Michigan

© 2017 by John M. Perkins

Published by Baker Books
a division of Baker Publishing Group
PO Box 6287, Grand Rapids, MI 49516-6287
www.bakerbooks.com

Paper edition published 2018
ISBN 978-0-8010-7586-5

Printed in the United States of America

The Library of Congress has cataloged the original edition as follows:
Names: Perkins, John, 1930– author.
Title: Dream with me : race, love, and the struggle we must win / John M. Perkins.
Description: Grand Rapids : Baker Books, 2017. | Includes bibliographical references.
Identifiers: LCCN 2016031071 | ISBN 9780801007781 (cloth)
Subjects: LCSH: Perkins, John, 1930– | African Americans—Civil rights—History—20th century. | African American clergy—Biography. | African American civil rights workers—Mississippi—Biography. | African Americans—Civil rights—Mississippi—History—20th century. | Civil rights movements—Mississippi—History—20th century. | Mississippi—Race relations—History—20th century. | Civil rights—Religious aspects—Christianity—History—20th century. | Race relations—Religious aspects—Christianity—History—20th century. | Civil rights movements—United States—History—20th century.
Classification: LCC E185.61 .P433 2017 | DDC 323.092 [B]—dc23
LC record available at https://lccn.loc.gov/2016031071

In keeping with biblical principles of creation stewardship, Baker Publishing Group advocates the responsible use of our natural resources. As a member of the Green Press Initiative, our company uses recycled paper when possible. The text paper of this book is composed in part of post-consumer waste.

20 21 22 23 24   7 6 5 4 3

green press INITIATIVE

To those who continue to believe
that multiethnic churches are possible
and to every person who ever has
or will participate
in the CCDA movement and has accepted
the Three Rs and eight key components
as integral parts of your ministry.
Thank you all.

Contents

Contents

Appreciation

My good friend Jon Foreman, of the band Switchfoot, read my first book, *Let Justice Roll Down*, and was inspired to write a song about my life. When I asked him about it, these were his words:

"The Sound (John M. Perkins' Blues)" is a very important song for us as a band. I see so much hatred and fear around me. I see so many people living out their pain. I hear it on the radio. I see it in the headlines. John Perkins' story needs to be heard. This song was inspired by a man who sang a louder song than hatred. In a world where we are defined by our differences, Mr. Perkins' life of service and compassion is a tangible demonstration of what it means to live a life of love. Love is the loudest song we could sing. Louder than racism. Louder than fear. Louder than hatred. John Perkins said it right: love is the final fight. We're excited to hear this song on the radio, louder than pain.

Today I hope to return the favor, because Switchfoot's song has inspired me to tell a little bit more of my own story—this time through the lens of their lyrics, "Love is the final fight."

Foreword

Dream with Me is wonderful. I read, loved, and highly recommend it. The book speaks for itself, but far more if you know the man behind it. So it's John Perkins and how he's influenced me that I want to talk about. Mine is only one story. Thousands, if given the chance, would gladly tell their stories about John—and one day, at great banquets with Christ at the head of the table, they will.

There aren't many people—other than Jesus and my wife—who I can say changed my life. John Perkins is one of them.

In 1976, I read *Let Justice Roll Down*. It stunned me. In the book I learned that in 1946, when John was sixteen, his brother Clyde was shot and killed by a deputy sheriff while waiting for a theater to open. Twenty years later, John spoke out for voter registration and took on segregation when he enrolled his son Spencer in an all-white high school. After organizing a boycott, he was arrested. His beloved wife, Vera Mae, and his children, who were outside the Mississippi jail, heard him beaten and tortured.

I knew all this from reading that powerful book. But in 1988, I met John when both of us were speaking at a writers' conference. I took him to lunch and asked him questions. He told me he had dropped out of school in the third grade, but our coffee cups weren't half empty before I realized he was one of the wisest men I'd ever met. John smiled a lot and then shed a tear. When he crossed his legs, his raised pant leg revealed a sizable scar. I don't know whether that scar was old or new, temporary or permanent, from an accident or surgery or torture—but to me it symbolized what he'd endured and gave power to his words about forgiveness.

I'm not easily impressed, but after two hours I knew John Perkins was the real deal. Jesus came "full of grace and truth" (John 1:14 NKJV). Christ's fingerprints were all over John. He could have been angry and bitter; instead, he embodied gospel grace. He was incredibly kind to me, a thirty-four-year-old white suburban pastor trying to understand the world. Jesus flipped a switch in me that day, as he has with countless others who've hung out with John.

A year later, not coincidentally, I became involved in peaceful, nonviolent civil disobedience, modeled after the civil rights movement. This resulted in multiple arrests, brief jail stays, the loss of my job, and decidedly unpopular news coverage. The cause was different (defending the rights of unborn children), but as Martin Luther King Jr. put it, "Injustice anywhere is a threat to justice everywhere."

When arrests and lawsuits kept me from continuing as a pastor, I started a ministry that gave away all my book royalties to kingdom causes. Besides missions, pro-life work, and helping the poor, some of my other central concerns were racial justice and reconciliation. This came about because of John's influence, and I've been honored to support the John and Vera Mae Perkins Foundation for Reconciliation, Justice, and Christian Community Development.

When writing my novel *Dominion* in 1995, I made my main character a black journalist who grew up in Mississippi. I immersed myself in black history and interviewed many African Americans (including Reggie White, who was then playing for the Green Bay Packers). I contacted John's son Spencer, who lived in Jackson with the family of Chris Rice, a white brother. Chris and Spencer had coauthored *More Than Equals*, a book on racial reconciliation that I really appreciated.

I asked if I could meet with them and ended up in their home with their families.

I attended a Christian Community Development Association National Conference where John Perkins spoke. That afternoon as he walked me down the streets of Jackson, stories overflowed from his heart and mind. He took me into a thrift shop where he found an old hat that was tagged for twenty-five cents. He tried it on and asked for my verdict. I told him it looked snazzy. I'll never forget his delight at that treasure he'd found!

The girl at the counter recognized John as the founder of the ministry that owned the thrift shop and said, "Dr. Perkins, you shouldn't pay for that!" He insisted and then handed her the quarter and proudly put on his hat. I smiled every time I looked at him the rest of the day. What great happiness this man found in something so small—he saw life crowded with God's kindnesses, which helped me see the same.

My favorite character in my novels is Obadiah Abernathy, who played baseball in the old Negro leagues. He modeled dignity, grace, wisdom, and humor. My sports inspiration for Obadiah was Buck O'Neil of the Kansas City Monarchs, but my spiritual inspiration was John Perkins. Whenever I wrote dialogue for Obadiah, I asked myself, *What would John say?*

In 2008, the Evangelical Christian Publishers Association honored John Perkins with the Jordon Lifetime Achievement Award. I canceled whatever was on my schedule to attend the event at which he was presented with the award. After John spoke, I waited at a distance. Though ten years had passed since we'd last seen each other, his face lit up when he saw me, and he called me by name. A photographer snapped a picture of John greeting me, his hand on my shoulder, which appeared on the front page of a newspaper the next day. I still treasure that photo.

There's so much good in *Dream with Me*, because it flows straight out of John's heart. It's honest, humble, prophetic, and Christ-honoring. We need to hear it.

John, you've shown me Jesus. Countless people would say the same. I look forward to spending time together on God's new earth, where love, justice, and joy will be the air we breathe (see 2 Pet. 3:13).

Meanwhile, you have my heartfelt gratitude, brother. I'm encouraged by the words I believe Jesus will one day say to you: "Well done, my good and faithful servant."

Randy Alcorn
Author of *Dominion*; *Heaven*;
Money, Possessions, and Eternity;
and *If God Is Good*

Acknowledgments

I am incredibly grateful for those who have contributed to making this book a reality. I owe great thanks to:

- Steve Lawson, who listened to my voice and my stories and laid a foundation to make this book possible.
- Maria Bertoia for your willingness to sit with me, take notes, and begin to shape this story.
- Jannie Johnson for helping to ensure that my culture and history were represented well.
- Sarah Stripp for all of the hours we spent together researching, rewriting, and making this book what it is today.
- Linda Buford-Burks, editor/publisher of *HUSH Magazine* and owner of Rapha Communications LLC, for helping with the final editing to get *Dream with Me* to the publishers.
- The wonderful team at Baker Books, including Chad Allen, Amy Ballor, and Rebecca Cooper, for your editorial skills and for working hard to make this book happen.

God bless you all! *Dream with Me* would not have come to fruition without your skills and expertise.

Introduction

At eighty-six years old, people tell you how much wisdom you have. I don't know about all of that, but I do know that God has done much in me and through me, and He's still working on me.

I never set out to record the events of my life—not on paper or on film or in some university's archives. Truth be told, I have forgotten more of what has happened than I can remember. I like it that way because I always seek to focus on God giving me new dreams. But as I talk and teach—and anyone who knows me well knows I love to do both—I have found myself reflecting, digging deeper, and reaching a few conclusions that have surprised even me.

I have always been a dreamer. It almost seems as if my life has gone back and forth between two worlds: the world that reflects reality around me and the world made by the dream I had of what life could be. My wife, Vera Mae, would always tell me to be careful because I would make people believe that the dream was already reality. When I was young, my dream was to get out of Mississippi and find a better life in California. After coming to know Jesus Christ and doing ministry in prisons with young men who looked like me and spoke the same broken English, I began to dream again. I dreamed of going back to my home state of Mississippi and sharing the love and joy of Jesus Christ that I had discovered in California.

I have continued to seek to live out that dream in my life—to fulfill the Great Commission—but I hope the dream world I long for now looks like the coming kingdom of God.

As much as we need to dream, we must also never forget what has happened in the past. We know how much farther we can go partly by seeing and marveling at how far God has already brought us. I have never stopped being amazed by God's redemptive love and His willingness to allow us to participate in spreading that love. To think of what God has done for me—a poor, third-grade dropout from rural Mississippi—is truly amazing, and every day I have to recognize that all of what I have done and have been given is by God's grace alone.

It's thrilling to actually see happening what so many of us have been working toward for more than half a century—more freedom, more justice, and more love. So here, I glance over my shoulder not simply to rehash old news but as a way to push onward. I offer reflections on some small steps my friends and I have taken with God and ponder some big struggles we all face today as individuals, as the church, and as a nation. These are my memories, insights, and dreams, as well as some confessions. As I grow older, I think I become more and more aware of my own sinfulness and the sin that is all around me. But what a joy it is to offer up my confessions to God, knowing that I am forgiven and saved by His grace. I don't want to pretend that I have lived a perfect life, and I hope this book will remind every reader that all the good that has been done through my life has been by God's grace and not my own works.

—⁂—

Like many couples, Vera Mae and I watch the news on television. I often read the newspaper too—yes, I am what younger generations call "old school," but I like the smell of newsprint and the sound of pages crinkling. We see the same stories you see—a tornado devastates a small town in Nebraska; the threat of war simmers in a foreign country; another business fails; yet another Hollywood marriage gets messy; congressional approval ratings fall; hate crimes continue to rage in relation to ethnicity and religion; and in my hometown of Jackson, Mississippi, paramedics rush a pregnant teenage girl to a hospital after a drive-by, drug-related shooting—and we start to wonder if society has really come all that far. As I look back on my life, I see the many successes that have happened in my lifetime. But justice is something for which every generation has to strive. I may have helped win some victories for my generation, but it is time for the next generations to pick up the mantle and continue the fight. True justice isn't something we will see until the kingdom of God comes in its fullness. And until that day, we will call those under us to keep striving to right the wrongs for their own generation.

In many ways, our nation appears to be more divided and hateful than ever. Stereotyping, profiling, race-baiting, and dehumanizing those we consider to be "different" from us mark our country instead of the grace and love we are called to demonstrate as Christians. Those of us in the older generations bear this cross. Yet as I travel from city to city, I hear a very different story from a small but growing number of young people, mostly college students and recent graduates. Their fervent passion, belief in change, and acceptance of one another have convinced me that America stands at the doorstep of a potentially historic and profound breakthrough for blacks, whites, Latinos, and everyone. I contend that these young men and women are the ones to take up the call for justice for their generation.

—⟋⟍—

I tend to speak more Mississippi Ebonics than Ivy-League English, so I have asked my editors to *craft* (their word!) sentences and paragraphs that reflect my heart, but they also have agreed to let me keep my speaking voice throughout. So the result is a mixture. I like that. As you mull over what I have written, done, and dreamed, I hope you will say, "John Perkins tried to live out a Christian life in the days in which he lived." That's all. Just that I did my best to be faithful with what God has given me in the days He has allotted me.

This book is part of my attempt to do just that. So together, let's dream a little . . .

Prologue

Unexpected Places

My grandson Big John and I made good time on the interstate. The slight drizzle that tailed us for most of the 188-mile drive south from Jackson held off until we reached New Orleans, where it became real rain, clickety-clacking on the hood of our car like a band of tap dancers in the French Quarter. Big John turned the wipers to fast, and we swished our way through the final few blocks to our hotel.

In a way, the downpour and clogged streets were a fitting welcome. You see, the Big Easy has always made me a little uneasy, though I am no stranger there. No doubt the voodoo underbelly and nonstop carnival mood feed my anxiousness. But I would like to think I am also moved by the pain I feel for my folks there: the poor who don't know they are poor and the downhearted who are still staggering years after the devastation of Hurricane Katrina.

Most visitors come to New Orleans to have a good time. Not me. It seems I always come on serious business, and this trip on a rainy day in November was no exception. An hour or so after we checked in to the Marriott, Big John and I found two empty, cushy chairs in the lobby. Finally, we could relax. As we sat and chatted, hundreds of people whirled past. Some, like me, were in town for a conference of evangelical theologians; others had come to enjoy the jazz music or some Cajun cooking. I looked Big John square in the eyes and asked, "How in the world did I get *here?*"

At some point, we all ask this same question—or something like it. *What am I doing walking down the aisle to get married? Why was I asked to teach the Sunday school class? How did I end up living on the most dangerous street in the city? Why does justice matter to me?* The unexpected is precisely that: something we did not foresee or pursue, or an event or circumstance that unfolds in a surprising way. It may be an "aha!" moment or a sudden tragedy, an honor we never imagined or a challenge we never believed we'd be able to overcome. Whatever the specifics might be, these moments have a way of getting our hearts pumping and our nerves on edge—whether from joy, sadness, hope, or fear. They also have a way of defining our lives.

I've found myself in a lot of unexpected places—so many, in fact, that the question "How in the world did I get here?" has become a thread that runs throughout my story, just as much as justice and love run through it. As you read on, you will see what I mean.

—m—

I dropped out of school somewhere between the third and fifth grade, but now I have thirteen honorary doctorates. Colleges and seminaries invite me to speak to their students. And I have an academic center and two scholarship programs that bear my name.

I was sixteen when a white deputy sheriff shot and killed my twenty-five-year-old brother, Clyde, in New Hebron, Mississippi, where we had grown up. Clyde had returned home from fighting in World War II just six months earlier after being honorably discharged from the army, with combat ribbons to show for it. He and his girlfriend, Elma, were waiting in a long line with other blacks for the movie theater ticket booth to open (whites got their tickets at a separate booth in another area of the theater). The crowd was a bit noisy, and the deputy sheriff had instructed everyone more than once to be quiet.

Clyde and Elma, who were turned away from the sheriff, were talking, when the officer clubbed Clyde over the head. Clyde grabbed the deputy sheriff's blackjack—probably an automatic reaction intensified by his military training—and struggled with him. The officer took two steps back, pulled his gun, and shot Clyde twice in the stomach. The local doctor tried to tend to his wounds, but what he could do was limited. So my family carefully placed Clyde into my cousin's '41 Chevy and headed to the nearest hospital in Jackson. Clyde's life was drifting away as he continued to bleed during the entire car ride. He was taken to a treatment room at the hospital and some time later officially declared dead. My big brother, a heroic survivor of World War II, was defeated by the unspoken war at home. I was devastated. I was the youngest sibling and looked up to him more than my other siblings (Clifton, Mary, and Emma Jean).

My family sent me from Mississippi to California, fearing that I would meet the same fate as my brother if I stayed. To them, it looked like I might not make it out of my teens. As I write this book, I'm eighty-six years old, and I've celebrated sixty-five years of marriage and fifty-six years of Christian ministry.

When I was a boy, I was paid fifteen cents for a hard day's work hauling hay. Decades later, a just-elected United States president asked me for advice on how justice is an economic issue. As a civil rights worker in the '60s and early '70s, I was arrested and beaten for fighting for freedom in rural Mississippi. Twenty years later, I found myself on a stage just to the left of President Ronald Reagan when he gave his "Evil Empire" speech.

How in the world did all this happen?

I've traveled the world to cities such as Beijing, Tokyo, São Paulo, Sydney, Nairobi, London, and all the major cities in the United States, preaching about the human race, freedom, and faith. I have shared meals and conversations with governors, billionaires, sports stars, university presidents, megachurch pastors, and all sorts of so-called movers and shakers. I have received pats on the back, accolades, and praise. I have written books, been interviewed on television, and even served on prestigious boards and panels.

I am tremendously grateful for these opportunities and for the wonderful people I've met along the way. But deep down inside, I'm still the kid who grew up in a family of sharecroppers and bootleggers in a small town in the Deep South. I'm still most comfortable picking greens with my childhood friend Ed, chatting with a single mother while waiting in line at Popeyes, or sitting on the steps of a row-house porch in Philadelphia with my friend Shane and some of his young neighbors as we enjoy a sunny afternoon together and wipe ice cream from the kids' faces. While I appreciate the attention I've gotten for my work and the kind words people have said about me, the look you see on my face most often is not so much one of accomplishment but, rather, one of astonishment.

How in the world did I get here?

The only answer I know to give is that these things can happen when you walk with God. It's easy to look at a person—to see where he started and how far he has come—and think you know how the story will end. But I've learned what Saul learned on the road to Damascus: when God's involved, everything can change in an instant. You may think you know where you're headed, but often God has a different plan—something "exceedingly abundantly above all that [you] ask or think" (Eph. 3:20 NKJV). Sometimes a light drizzle becomes a deluge. Other times you open your eyes to find yourself by still waters. Sometimes you hear thunder clapping along with the rain. Other times the clouds disappear so you can see a billion stars in the sky.

Just when I think I've witnessed every possible thing, something else comes along. Sort of like a rainbow appearing after a lightning storm. On the last night of that conference in New Orleans, a popular band called Switchfoot performed at the House of Blues, just a few blocks from the Marriott where I was staying. The music was too loud for my ears, but my daughter Elizabeth and one of our interns,

Nikki, went. Switchfoot's set included a song they say was inspired by my first book, *Let Justice Roll Down*. And, yes, Switchfoot put my name in the song title: "The Sound (John M. Perkins' Blues)."[1]

Now, how did *that* happen?

—⚬⚬—

Anyone who knows my story would expect this book to ooze with justice issues. After all, the pain caused by injustice has motivated me to spend a lifetime working for social change on behalf of widows, prisoners, the poor, and anyone who struggles. So how did someone who has experienced the anguish of poverty, racism, and oppression end up wanting to write a book about love as his climactic message? Good question.

For decades I've tried to meet people where they hurt. I've preached and desired to see "justice for all," and I still fervently believe in it. God loves justice and wants His people to seek justice (see Ps. 11 and Mic. 6:8). But I've come to understand that true justice is wrapped up in love. The old-time preacher and prophet A. W. Tozer had a way of making the most profound truths simple and palatable. He once said, "God is love, and just as God is love, God is justice."[2] That's it! God's love and justice come together in the redemptive work of Jesus Christ, and we can't be about one and not the other. They're inextricably connected.

God is holy and just. He is life. He is light. He is love. When we try to understand people's actions, whether at a crime scene or just in everyday life, the most important thing to look for is their motivation. John 3:16 tells us that because God so loved the world He sent His only Son to save us. Love is what brought God down from heaven and generated the incarnation. Love was always God's motivation, which is why it must be ours as well.

As I think about what I want to say to people—from a pulpit, in a book, at the dinner table, in the lobby of a Marriott, or in line at Popeyes—at this point in my life, it's all about love. As I look back over my personal journey—the highs, the lows, and everything in between—it's all about love. Love is the first, middle, *and* final fight.

We live in a broken world. How should we react? No doubt, some actions lessen the pain—and that's a good thing. But neither clenched fists nor helping hands alone will bring about the complete transformation God wants. Only love can touch us at the point of our pain and begin to heal us and make us whole—individually and collectively. We are called to love. To love God, to love our neighbors, even to love our enemies. Yes, love can be a real struggle. Anger is easier. Even a tireless, lifelong campaign for justice might be simpler.

I often tell people that justice is a stewardship and economic issue, but truthfully, I think love is as well. Justice and love are intimately tied together in this way. Caring for those who have the least, loving our neighbors as we love ourselves, showing mercy to those around us—these are all issues of love, but they are also issues of justice. We cannot have true justice unless it is motivated by love, just as God's greatest act of justice, sending Jesus to die for us, was motivated by love.

Years ago, before the emancipation of slaves, Frederick Douglass described the contradiction and failure of the church in America, saying:

> Fellow-citizens, I will not enlarge further on your national inconsistencies. The existence of slavery in this country brands your republicanism as a sham, your humanity as a base pretense, and your Christianity as a lie. It destroys your moral power abroad: it corrupts your politicians at home. It saps the foundation of religion; it makes your name a hissing and a bye-word to a mocking earth. It is the antagonistic force in your government, the only thing that seriously disturbs and endangers your Union. It fetters your progress; it is the enemy of improvement; the deadly foe of education; it fosters pride; it breeds insolence; it promotes vice; it shelters crime; it is a curse to the earth that supports it; and yet you cling to it as if it were the sheet anchor of all your hopes. Oh! be warned! be warned! a horrible

reptile is coiled up in your nation's bosom; the venomous creature is nursing at the tender breast of your youthful republic; for the love of God, tear away, and fling from you the hideous monster, and let the weight of twenty millions crush and destroy it forever![3]

Today I fear we can say the same thing in regard to the racism that is still deeply ingrained in the church in America, and I think I can use these same words as an indictment of the church today. But it is time to repent. It is time to forgive. It is time to move forward from the racism and bigotry that we have allowed to define us for too long. It is time for love, rather than pride and division, to be our final fight.

1

Side by Side
(but Not Together)

Desegregation was one of the big goals of the civil rights movement. "Separate but equal" in the South became "separate and unequal." The disparities were in things as small as water fountains and as vitally important as education and health care.

In fact, when we black patients were sick, we had trouble getting to see a doctor. We had to be to the doctor's office by 8:00 a.m., because if we weren't, other black patients would get there first, and we might not get to see the doctor that day. If a doctor did see us, it would always be in the afternoon after the white patients had left. People would sit all day at the doctor's office and still not see the doctor that day. Our time meant nothing to them.

In the case of an accident, or if the doctor had to rush to the hospital, none of us black patients got treated. We had to return the next day and start over again. Appointments didn't exist for blacks.

My son Phillip had polio as a child, and we learned that we could get some of his medication through the March of Dimes. They told us they had a representative in every county and sent us to a health clinic in downtown Mendenhall, Mississippi.

We had to go in through a back door and wait for hours in a separate waiting room to get my little boy's medicine. I didn't think about it too much. That's the way things were, and the important thing was to take care of Phillip.

In the years since then, I often have thought about those walls that kept black people and white people apart, even in places where we had so much in common. And yet we were treated as if we were two different species.

—⚹—

In 1973, Voice of Calvary Ministries, the ministry Vera Mae and I started after we moved back to Mississippi in 1960, opened a health clinic in the black section of Mendenhall. We had an X-ray machine and all new equipment. We were thrilled about our clinic, but we had barely gotten it open before a terrible flood caused thousands of dollars of damage to our equipment and the facility. We needed to find a location on higher ground.

The white doctor who had run the clinic up by the courthouse had died, and according to his wishes, his widow was to sell the building only to someone who would use it as a medical clinic. The property was located uptown, in the white section of town, and no property had ever been sold to a black person there before. The widow sold us the building because we convinced her we were committed to using it to provide health care for the community.

I'll never forget the day we took possession of that building. We paid her $75,000 cash, and she deeded the clinic over to Voice of Calvary.

As soon as we had the keys, a bunch of us went inside. The first thing I noticed was the wall that divided blacks and whites. Many times I had stared at the wall from the black side. For the first time, we were able to look at both sides of the wall, and it confirmed what we had already assumed: the white side had nice, beautiful paneling; the black side was bare and worn.

34

The stark contrast was symbolic of how everything we blacks had was inferior.

I picked up a sledgehammer and started slamming it against the wall with all my might. We tore down that dividing wall in less than thirty minutes. It felt good! It also reminded me of something the apostle Paul wrote in Ephesians 2:14–16: Christ has made peace between Jews and gentiles, and He has united us by breaking down the wall of hatred that separated us.

It was an emotional experience, and I didn't care that we had ruined nice paneling that, under other circumstances, we would have reused. From that time on, we determined there would be only one waiting room—open to blacks and whites.

At our new clinic, all patients came in through the same door and sat in the same waiting room until a doctor was ready to see them. From the beginning, even some poor whites used our clinic.

The first physician to work at the clinic was Dr. Kevin Lake. For a while volunteer doctors came to help out for a few months or a year or two. Dr. Gene McCarty was the clinic's first full-time doctor. He stayed for two years and helped expand the clinic's capacity as a medical facility. Dr. Dennis Adams, a young black man from New York, joined the clinic staff because he felt God was calling him to serve with us in Mississippi. He's been at the clinic for more than forty years. He and his wife raised their kids in Mendenhall. People love him. He has black and white patients.

When I visit Mendenhall, I love to watch people going into that integrated clinic. I smile because it's in the shadow of the courthouse.

Tearing down the wall in that health center was for me what refusing to give up her seat on that bus must have been for Rosa Parks. That is something I look back on and think, *Because of what we did, things are different. Life is better now.*

To this day, every time I see the building, it brings me great joy to know that the wall that once separated the races came tumbling down.

— row—

Discrimination was prominent in restaurants, hotels, and bus depots. Black citizens weren't allowed to participate in the society they had spent centuries helping build.

Segregation was wrong, so we fought it with all we had.

In 1968, civil rights hero Andrew Young, who stood on the balcony with Martin Luther King Jr. when he was killed, spoke at Jackson State University, a historically black university. The organizers printed 3,000 posters promoting the event. The auditorium where Mr. Young spoke could seat about 1,500 people.

Fewer than 400 attended. About 250 came from the community, leaving about 150 students from a campus of 3,700 undergraduate and graduate students. I don't blame the students for not coming. I blame the professors for not making the event a priority.

Two days before Christmas in 1969, I was jailed for protesting the beating of a black boy who supposedly telephoned a white girl to ask her for a date. Vera Mae helped organize a shopping boycott of white-owned stores in Mendenhall to protest. In February of the following year, I went to the Rankin County Jail in Brandon to visit nineteen Tougaloo college students who had been arrested after a protest march. I was subsequently arrested and tortured by white police officers. We as a society have failed the students of today if they don't understand and respect the leaders and martyrs who worked tirelessly for the cause of equality.

Courageous men, women, and children who were willing to give their lives for the cause of equality led the civil rights movement. Young people were often the hands and feet behind the vision of the adult leaders. They made sacrifices and provided energy for the movement.

I'll never forget one Sunday in 1964 when a bunch of kids met up together and decided they were going to integrate the movie theater in Mendenhall. This was fairly early on in the integration efforts, but they had a pretty good idea that integrating meant going to jail and getting beaten up.

The kids tried to keep it a secret because they knew their parents wouldn't want them involved. But word got out, sending numerous parents into a fearful panic. They feared not only for their children's safety but also for their own livelihoods. People whose kids went to jail for trying to integrate a whites-only facility risked losing their jobs, their insurance, and their homes.

I attended the meeting, not to try to talk them out of anything, but to listen. My eldest children—Spencer, Joanie, Phillip, and Derek— were there. Vera Mae and I wanted the kids to go even though, like the other parents, we were concerned for their safety. We didn't have to worry about the other threats because we didn't work for white folks, the bank didn't have a lien on our house, and our insurance agent was a fairly decent white man.

At the meeting, I listened to the organizer talk to the kids. He told them the truth—they might go to jail, get beaten, or, worst of all, killed.

Finally, he said, "It's time to go." The way he said those words was as powerful as if he were saying, "Even if no one comes with me, I'm going."

As I recall, Spencer, who wasn't more than eleven at the time, was the first to stand and go with him. (Although it may have been Joanie—she was always a rebel.) Derek also was a rebel, and Phillip would do anything Spencer did. All four of my children, along with fourteen others, tried to integrate the theater.

That event was a pivotal moment in my life. I had to make a choice, and that choice revealed a lot about who I am. *If my kids are ready to give their lives for the cause, I'm willing to let them do it.* Some parents might not have agreed with that decision, but my children understood that some ideals are important enough to risk their lives for.

I was proud of them for that stance.

The theater owners must have also recognized the determination of these young protesters. When they heard the kids were coming, they closed the theater.

Permanently.

—◊◊◊—

Not long ago, I went back to Mendenhall and crossed paths with Bettye Norwood, who had been part of our ministry. After being employed with World Vision in California for twenty years, she came back home and worked in the Simpson County district attorney's office.

When she was growing up, it was unheard of for a black woman to have such a position. "I never thought that I would be in this courthouse working with a top official," she said.

As we talked, we reminisced about the time a group of us integrated a local truck stop.

I was terrified, but I was the leader, so I tried not to let it show.

The employees at the truck stop finally decided to serve us, and we sat while they put the plates and forks in front of us. I tried to pick up my fork, but I was shaking so badly, I couldn't do it.

Afterward, people asked me, "What did you do?"

"We integrated. That's what we went there to do."

Fear or no fear, we had made up our minds that we were going to keep pressing on until we were allowed to sit at tables just like the white people.

If you want to see how much Mississippi has changed in the last fifty years, look at the restaurants. Pictures of the group that integrated the Woolworth's lunch counter in downtown Jackson back in 1963 remain etched in my mind.

"A huge mob gathered, with open police support while the three of us sat there for three hours," a member of that group, former Tougaloo College sociology professor John Salter, said. "I was attacked with fists, brass knuckles and the broken portions of glass sugar containers, and was burned with cigarettes."[1]

A few blocks from the location of that Woolworth's is Hal and Mal's. The place features live music and is regularly filled with both black and white customers. A few blocks in the other direction is the King Edward Hotel, which reminds me how far we've come.

According to the *Jackson Free Press*,

> Built in 1922, the current iteration of the hotel was a favorite watering hole for white state legislators and other dealmakers during the days of Prohibition and after. The hotel fell on hard times midway through the 1950s, and the King Edward remained segregated after other downtown hotels integrated. When it finally began admitting black guests, the hotel's remaining white patrons jumped ship, and in 1967, the King Edward closed its doors.[2]

In 2009, the hotel reopened after the building was renovated by a group of investors, including a white attorney, a black professional athlete, and a black rap artist. In the remodeled building, anyone can rent apartments, stay in hotel rooms, and eat at the restaurant, bar, and coffee shop. This truly is a testament to progress and transformation.

—⁘—

I like to talk about the positive changes of integration. However, it's harder to talk about the costs and unintended effects. Take, for example, the schools.

Six of my children—Spencer, Joanie, Phillip, Derek, Deborah, and Wayne—were among the first black children to attend the all-white school in Mendenhall. But while they were there, their white teachers did not treat them the same way they treated the white children.

Phillip's teacher wouldn't allow him to answer questions in class. For two years Spencer went to the school and no one talked to him. The seat next to him was always left empty, and as far as people at school were concerned, both his first and last name were a racial slur.

Whenever one of my kids did make a white friend, it wasn't long before that friend would come to school and say, "My parents said I can't play with you anymore."

Phillip was probably hurt the most by his school experience. Because he was sickly, I had always given him a lot of love. He grew to expect that other people would love him too. When he went to the white school and the people treated him with hatred, the rejection almost destroyed him.

I didn't even know several of the stories until many years later because our children had tried to keep some of the hatred and rejection they had experienced from hurting me and Vera Mae too. Deborah remembers some of this well and says,

> My first day in class with all white students, I walked in and was assigned my seat. Of course, everyone was staring. Even the teacher seemed to be a little shaken presenting her lesson plan. Confidence was rarely a problem for me as a kid, with three athletic older brothers, but this day I was all alone. Not one student said a word to me, nor did I see a smile. It seemed that I could feel their eyes while reading their thoughts. I was alone on the playground. I ate lunch alone. If I got on the monkey bars, the kids got off. When I jumped on the merry-go-round, my classmates jumped off. I would hear people say, "My dad is going to kill your dad." This was my life in first grade, only six years old. The end of the day, the school bell would ring, and I would pack my books under my arm and walk toward the big magnolia tree where we were to be picked up and wait—alone.
>
> One afternoon, as I was standing there, two white older boys who must have been in third or fourth grade slapped my books out from under my arm. The books spread out on the ground. As I stood in slight shock, I told myself not to cry. Before I could bend down to pick up the books, the two white boys reached ahead of me and were starting to pick them up. As I glanced over my shoulder, I saw two of my older brothers standing behind me. I stepped back. The white boys picked up my books and returned them to me. My brother told me not to tell Mom and Dad about the bullies.

I sometimes question my motivation for letting my kids endure the kind of torment they experienced to desegregate the schools. Did I send them out of pride? Was I wrong to let them suffer for a cause I believed in? Maybe.

At the same time, it was the natural step to take as a leader. I was a leader in the movement, so shouldn't my family be pioneers in integration efforts? How could I ask other families to send their kids to those schools if I wouldn't send my own?

It was the right thing to do, but I'm still troubled at times. I put my children in harm's way.

It's also painful to think about the way the schools have resegregated themselves. And the church has helped.

When the federal government ordered desegregation, many white parents decided to keep their kids from going to school with black kids. During the first year of integration, they formed all-white private academies. After the government said that was illegal and wouldn't give them tax-exempt status, they turned the schools over to the churches.

Today the public school system in Jackson is about 98 percent black. Some of this resegregation came about simply because of where people live—after all, the population of Jackson is about 80 percent black. *But about 20 percent of Jackson's population is white.*[3]

So where are those white kids going to school? Most of them attend private Christian academies, many which were established in the '60s, after schools were forced to desegregate. Academically, these academies are among the best schools in Jackson, so I understand why parents want to send their children to them. I don't want to condemn that choice, and as I mentioned before, I still question my own choice to send my children to integrate the schools in the early '60s. I do not believe our children should be used to make political statements or pacify the guilt parents might feel about having the ability to send their children to better schools.

However, I also see an undermining of the purpose of integration, resulting from decisions to move children out of the public schools. The most obvious sign is a weakened resolve by the community to see that all children receive a top-notch education.

A separate and unequal education. Many Christians who send their kids to private schools don't understand how this decision affects the quality of education for black children. It's a major blind spot.

I want to make people aware of the effect this choice has on our black children in the public schools. It is still resegregation, which was proved by the Supreme Court in *Brown v. Board of Education* to be inherently unequal. If we continue to separate our children based on race and social status, particularly keeping poor blacks in inferior conditions, how can we ever expect them to learn to reconcile? It will just lead to more violence, hatred, and crime.

I pray that parents of schoolchildren will wrestle over their decision about where to send their kids to school and realize it's not just their children who are affected by their choices.

—⟋⟍—

Not long ago, I was invited to Mendenhall High School, which is truly integrated now. I told the students about myself, especially my conversion, my experience in Mendenhall, and how I spent eleven years working for civil rights in their hometown. When I finished, those kids broke into applause that went on for a long, long time.

After they were dismissed, many kids—both black and white—asked me to autograph anything they had in their hands. It was an emotional moment that made so much of the suffering and pain I had experienced disappear. The love they showed me testified to the redemptive work God has been doing in the community.

In Mendenhall, where the schools have actually integrated, we are seeing real equality form in the hearts of members of this new generation, and it is enriching for the entire community. When the schools stay separate, people in the community don't learn how to talk to one another. We don't learn to overcome our differences and get along. We don't learn to love. We may think we are keeping the peace by creating separate schools. In reality, we are taking away from a deeper peace that can come with developing close relationships with those of a different skin color.

A year after schools in Mendenhall became fully integrated, it came time to vote for the high school's homecoming queen. The school had about four hundred black students and only three hundred white students. Not surprisingly, a black girl won the title because of the majority of black students. The next day, though, the principal expelled the girl who had won, claiming she had once stolen from a white lady she had worked for years ago and was unfit for the title. However, the following day all of the black students stood up and walked out of the school in protest, along with a good number of the white students. The white teachers and principal may not have realized it, but a year of attending school together, playing basketball together, and learning to live and study with one another had changed those students' hearts. Integration may come with a cost, but when it leads to reconciliation, it is worth it.

—⁂—

Did desegregation fix all the racial problems in Mississippi or in America? No, it did not.

Did it change the world we live in for the better? Looking out at those kids at Mendenhall High, I believe it did.

Was it a goal worth the suffering and sacrifice? Everyone who participated in the effort has to answer that question for themselves, but for me, yes, it was.

Perhaps the best question to ask is, "Would you do that again?" The applause and the love and acceptance those children showed me would make me want to do it again. Yes, I would endure the pain and suffering for that redemptive, loving moment.

People like me, Martin Luther King Jr., and a few others sometimes earn a hero status for things we did during the civil rights movement, but really the daily, faithful acts of ordinary black and white folks made the movement what it was. The many people committed to marching and boycotting—who got no recognition but, rather, rocks thrown at them—were instrumental in tearing down the social walls of segregation. I am thankful for my chance to be a leader, but I cannot tell my story without acknowledging how much I depended on others. The names of many humble and courageous people might never be known, but the stories I tell are representative of their indelible work.

During the mid-1950s boycott in Montgomery, Mother Pollard, an old lady with blisters on her feet, was asked at the end of a march if she was tired. She responded by saying, "My feets is tired, but my soul is rested."[4] I think that is representative of how so many of us felt. The reality of life is that joy often comes out of pain and suffering—and that is the only way progress happens. While the pain was hard back then, I am thankful to have experienced some of the joy that has come out of it today.

2

That We Might Be One

It has often been said that church on Sunday morning is the most segregated time in America today. This rings true in Mississippi. We claim to be an ethnic "melting pot," yet people of different nationalities and backgrounds—black, white, Latino, Asian, Eastern European—most often worship with people who look, act, and talk like themselves. In His high priestly prayer in John 17, Jesus prayed that all the church might be one as He and the Father are one, as a witness to the world. Yet on Sunday morning, we seldom model this reality of the gospel.

Strong words? Yes. But I can't help but wonder how this division must displease God. How it must pain Him. As Bob Pierce, the founder of World Vision, used to say, "Let my heart be broken with the things that break the heart of God."

Reporters Alex Alston and James Dickerson tell a sad story about a church that sought to integrate its ranks:

> The Mississippi Delta was in a tizzy over rumors that blacks might show up at white churches to worship. Some white churches hired armed guards to keep them out. Other white churches considered allowing them to attend services. One Delta congregation, a Presbyterian

church with deep cultural roots, was split right down the middle. Half of the deacons voted no; the other half voted yes. After a contentious meeting to resolve the stalemate, one of the church elders hurriedly left the meeting to deliver the news to his mother, a firm believer in old-time segregation.

"Well, what did you decide?" she demanded.

"We decided to let them attend services."

"You know I'm very much opposed to that!"

"I know, Mother—but think about it this way. What would Jesus do?"

"I know good and well what He'd do," she huffed. "He'd say, let 'em in!"

She paused a moment, pondering the implications, then added, "But He'd be wrong!"[1]

Even though most Christians wouldn't make a statement as bold as the elder's mother, I don't think many Christians believe reconciliation and integrated worship are central to the gospel and to our lives as Christians. But it is. We need God's Word to help purge us of these sins that keep us apart. And it grieves and frightens me to the core to hear a Christian declare that maintaining racial separation is a higher value than imitating Christ!

—⁂—

Christ followers were first called Christians at Antioch—about fifteen years after the birth of the church at Pentecost. There must have been something remarkable about this particular group of believers—something that caught people's attention and caused them to come up with a new name for those who previously had been known simply as "Followers of the Way." What was happening at Antioch that was deserving of such special recognition?

Acts 13:1 lists some of the leaders of this church at Antioch, and if we pay attention, we see that these deacons and other leaders represented various ethnic groups. They came from very different backgrounds, but there they were, worshiping and serving God

46

together in equality. They were living out what Paul describes when he writes, "Therefore, if anyone is in Christ, he is a new creation; old things have passed away; behold, all things have become new!" (2 Cor. 5:17 NKJV), and "There is neither Jew nor Greek, there is neither slave nor free, there is neither male nor female; for you are all one in Christ Jesus" (Gal. 3:28 NKJV).

People—people I respect, people who are committed to reconciliation—disagree with me about this, but I am convinced that God's will is for churches to be integrated. When we come to worship God, we should gladly come into His presence alongside anyone else who has come to worship Him. But for the most part we have done something else instead. We have accommodated bigotry within the church. We have become captive to the same divisions and hostilities that have plagued our nation for generations. In fact, instead of leading our culture toward unity, love, and reconciliation, the church often lags behind secular efforts to promote equality and healing.

By continuing in this direction, the church weakens the power of the gospel and creates doubt as to whether the power of God as Paul describes it in Romans 1:16 can break down the walls between churches of various nationalities. This is the intention of the gospel—being reconciled to God and to one another. Second Corinthians 5:19 says this so clearly: "God was reconciling the world to himself in Christ, not counting people's sins against them. And he has committed to us the message of reconciliation." The church has been given the message of reconciliation. We are to proclaim it. If we are not reconciling, how can we call ourselves *the church*?

I'm not saying every single congregation comprised of only one race or ethnicity can't be the real church, but I do think that if we're not striving to integrate, we're ignoring what we have been told is the church's mission. The very essence of mission, as laid out by Jesus Christ in the Great Commission (see Matt. 28:19–20), is to share the gospel with every ethnic group. The end goal, then, is for all ethnic groups to be together in the family of God. If this is true, then why would we think that our local congregations shouldn't reflect that goal? If the kingdom of God is made up of every ethnic group, then let's start modeling that reality of the kingdom in our local congregations.

First John 3:18 reads, "Let us not love in word or in tongue, but in deed and in truth" (NKJV). We can pass lofty-sounding laws and give speeches about tolerance all day long. We can boast about how we have black or white, Native American or Persian friends, but as long as we do not worship together, it is only talk. Segregation in the church inhibits love, which is the gospel. How can we expect God to break down walls and be present among us when we will not do the same and be present among one another? This idea isn't new. If you have any doubts, read 1 John 3:11, which declares, "For this is the message that you heard from the beginning, that we should love one another" (NKJV).

—◊◊◊—

As I look out at the world today, I think we are in a situation similar to one Elijah experienced. Elijah was an Old Testament prophet during the reign of Ahab, perhaps the most wicked ruler in Israel's history. Ahab's wife, Jezebel, in particular, led the Israelites to worship Baal and killed many of the Lord's prophets so that Elijah was the only courageous prophet left. The people of Israel strayed so far from God that He sent a drought on the land for three years.

As God was about to lift the drought from Israel, He told Elijah to present himself to Ahab and show the people of Israel once again that He was the only true God. Most of us are probably familiar with the story of what followed. Elijah gathered the people of Israel, including 450 prophets of Baal, at Mount Carmel. Baal's prophets, after hours of shouting, dancing, and even violently beating themselves, were unable to call their god to bring down fire from heaven to consume the bull they had sacrificed. Elijah, however, said a prayer to God, who sent down fire to consume not only the altar and sacrificed bull—which Elijah had drenched with water—but also the water in the trench surrounding the altar. It was an awesome display of the power of God and the importance of serving Him alone (see 1 Kings 18:16–40).

Yet what happened next intrigues me the most. God had promised Elijah that if he presented himself to Ahab, He would lift the drought from the land. Elijah knew how desperately the land needed rain and how anxious the people were for food and drink. Elijah, on top of Mount Carmel, knelt down with his face to the ground, prayed for rain, and told his servant, "Go and look toward the sea" for a cloud or sign of rain. When the servant returned, he said he saw nothing. The servant went to look five more times but reported he saw nothing. Finally, on the seventh time, the servant returned and reported, "A cloud as small as a man's hand is rising from the sea." This was all Elijah needed. He then told Ahab to get his chariot ready because the rain was coming (see 1 Kings 18:41–46).

The cloud was as small as a man's hand, yet it gave him hope. I wonder if Elijah even believed that what the servant saw was a real cloud. Maybe he thought the servant's mind was playing tricks on him, or that after desperately searching the skies so many times, he had just imagined the small spot so that he could finally report something. But it was enough. It gave Elijah something to hold on to. It told Elijah that there was hope for Israel after all, that God had not abandoned His people despite their years of unfaithfulness. Wrapped up in that little cloud, Elijah saw the promise of God's steadfast love and His commitment to His people. He saw the Lord's new mercies about to be poured out on Israel. In that cloud, Elijah found the hope he needed to keep going.

I know most Americans today do not worship Baal, but when I look at the church in America, I fear that we have our own Baals that demand our worship. I see so many people bowing down before prosperity theology and the idea that God just wants to make us wealthy and happy. I see people entrapped by the "-isms"—racism, sexism, ageism, classism, and so many others—that divide our church, choosing first to obey and revere these divisive systems rather than the God who has called us to be reconciled to one another and to be one in Christ Jesus. Perhaps people today aren't declaring their allegiance quite as bluntly as the elder's mother in the Mississippi Delta story I told earlier, but as we look at our churches, we cannot deny that they are divided by ethnicity, class, and age. We surround ourselves with people who are like us and value like-mindedness over genuine love and care for our neighbor.

Yet I am starting to believe that I have seen my own cloud. It is still small, maybe no bigger than the size of a man's hand, but I think it is there. I see a movement of people excited and energized by multi-ethnic church planting, and that gives me so much hope. People all over the country are inviting me to conferences and churches that recognize diversity as a value, that are filled with people beginning to catch the vision of laying aside some of our differences to be united as one body. And this gives me hope. Let me tell you about just a few of the movements and churches I have grown to love.

—⚬—

Many people know me because I was part of the team that started the Christian Community Development Association (CCDA). At its start, CCDA was intended to be a network where people from across the country could come together, exchange ideas, and mutually support one another in the work of Christian community development. An essential part of this network was an annual conference that physically brought together all of these people.

CCDA started off with the three Rs—relocation, reconciliation, and redistribution—which I'll talk about more extensively in later chapters. However, as time went on, it became apparent that a few more principles were needed to help better explain the work of CCDA. This realization led to the development of five additional principles—leadership development, empowerment, listening to the community, holistic development, and striving to be church based. Over time, the nonprofit and parachurch worlds have been evolving into entities separate from the church, taking on outreach efforts and social justice concerns once addressed by the church. But as CCDA began to grow and develop, this work needed to be centered on the church. The church is to be the incarnated Christ here on earth now, which means all members ought to be doing the work Christ did while He was here.

As CCDA has grown to be more church based, I have started to see more young church planters and church members among the approximately three thousand attendees at the annual conference. While we talk about ways parachurch organizations can thrive, we also talk about ways we can more authentically live out our multiethnic faith. We spend time worshiping together in diverse styles of worship led by people of various ethnicities. We hear sermons and plenary sessions given by leaders of ethnicities. It is a true picture of multiethnic worship, and the people who attend love it. Many comment afterward that it is one of the greatest expressions of multiethnic worship they have ever experienced, and they hope to replicate it in their own churches.

I get so much energy from the young people at the conference who have caught the vision and are excited to help make their churches look a little bit more like the multiethnic, multiclass kingdom of God we know is coming. I have met people with a similar energy, who are part of the conferences for Verge Network, Mosaic, Kainos, and Catalyst. Others like these exist, and more are coming. Multiethnic in their focus, they represent "Elijah's hand" that's going to turn into a storm, as they organize and mobilize these young church planters to continue working with a fresh, new vision. These young people are excited to see change happening in the church and are invigorated by the opportunity to start gospel-centered churches that are free from the systems of discrimination and bigotry that have long stood as the backbone of the church in America. I always leave these conferences excited and hopeful, energized by the prospect that the church in America might finally be losing its chains of racism.

—ᴍ—

I have come to know some specific churches and pastors and have been inspired by their vision. Just a few hours north of where I live in Jackson, Mississippi, is Fellowship Memphis, a church striving to be both gospel-centered and ethnically diverse. Founded in 2003 by Dr. John W. Bryson and Bryan Loritts, Fellowship Memphis has, in many ways, become a thriving picture of what a multiethnic church can be. Like me, these men have a dream and a vision for the church to overcome the racism and bigotry that has long been a part of the history of Memphis. They describe their dream like this:

> We dream, even to the point of tears, to provide a medicating balm to the "black eye" of Memphis. From slavery to the assassination of Dr. King and beyond, Memphis has garnered the unfortunate reputation of racism. By standing on the authority of the Bible, and modeling diversity within our walls, we long to be a model to Memphians, the Mid-South and the world of diversity, racial reconciliation and racial harmony. To a world that says blacks and whites worshiping and doing life together in Memphis could never happen, we dream, labor and sacrifice all that we are by the power of the Holy Spirit and the authority of the blood of Jesus to say, "Yes it can! Yes it will!"[2]

Hearing people talk like this and actually begin to live it out in their church is what gives me hope. It allows me to believe that the work we have started is not in vain and that someday this dream will become a reality for all of us to see.

Another wonderful example of this happening is Quest Church in Seattle, Washington, started by my friend Eugene Cho. When Eugene and his wife, Minhee, first felt called to plant a multiethnic church in urban Seattle, they started as a house church. They eventually grew, joined the Evangelical Covenant denomination, and became a multiethnic church community, striving to be actively involved in the Seattle area. That alone is a great story, but it gets better.

Quest Church was a young, hip church with a coffee shop, and they did concerts and met in a warehouse owned by another congregation, Interbay Covenant Church. Quest Church was trendy and cool, but most members of the congregation were in their twenties and the atmosphere definitely appealed to only a certain demographic. Interbay Covenant Church, located right across the parking lot, had a very different congregation. It was well-established and mostly comprised of older people and families who had been a part of the church for a long time. However, after a few years, both churches began to realize that if they were to be a true reflection of the multiethnic, multigenerational kingdom of God, they needed to find a way to worship together instead of just next to each other.

After much prayer and some tense moments, Interbay Covenant Church offered to give their facilities to Quest Church and merge together to be one church. Quest is now a multiethnic, multigenerational church that is continuing to grow. People of various ages are inspired by a church that preaches a gospel that is bigger than the barriers we have allowed to divide us for far too long. Churches like Quest give me hope for the church of the future.

—⁘—

I think one of the most beautiful passages in the Bible is found in Revelation 7:9–12. It says,

> After these things I looked, and behold, a great multitude which no one could number, of all nations, tribes, peoples, and tongues, standing before the throne and before the Lamb, clothed with white robes, with palm branches in their hands, and crying out with a loud voice, saying, "Salvation belongs to our God who sits on the throne, and to the Lamb!" All the angels stood around the throne and the elders

and the four living creatures, and fell on their faces before the throne and worshiped God, saying:

> "Amen! Blessing and glory and wisdom,
> Thanksgiving and honor and power and might,
> Be to our God forever and ever.
> Amen." (NKJV)

All nations, tribes, peoples, and tongues will be together, praising and worshiping God in unity. I long for the day when this vision becomes reality. I long for a kingdom in which we aren't divided over issues of culture or hatred of the past. I hear people arguing about everything from church pews to worship songs to old cultural traditions, but we need to start getting beyond this stuff. Acts 17:26 declares that the people from every nation are "made from one blood" (NKJV), so we are all one race. Issues related to ethnicity and tribalism may divide us, but we have to start recognizing that we are one race —the human race. The problems that divide us are surmountable.

We have been given a clear picture of what this kingdom is to look like—multiethnic, multicultural, multigenerational, multiclass—and we need to be on the side of that coming kingdom now. No, we are no longer in a society in which white church councils have meetings about whether to even let black people enter the doors, but we still live in a time when the majority of churches today do not look anything like John's vision in Revelation. But people like Bryan and Eugene give me hope that we might become one as Jesus prayed we would. Their thriving congregations and the many people catching hold of their visions remind me that there is a cloud coming up over the lake, even if it is only the size of a man's hand. The people who gather together and worship at CCDA and the energetic church planters who are part of these other conferences show me that the rain is coming. And be prepared for when it does, because if it is anything like what happened in Elijah's day, this little cloud is about to take over the entire sky—and the heavy rain will come.

3

Poor Whites

When my family and a team of us from the Mendenhall ministry moved to Jackson in 1972, we purchased several buildings, including a rundown house in one of the roughest and poorest neighborhoods in town, not far from where I live today. The old house was very big, and we called it the Samaritan Inn. The idea was for it to be a temporary place to stay for people who were visiting from out of town or didn't have a place to live or were stuck because their car broke down. It wasn't so much a shelter as it was a guesthouse.

We negotiated a low price for the house, but it was rather messy and would have been a good candidate for one of those extreme home makeover shows if there had been such a show back then. There wasn't, so we turned to our good friends Paul House and Cal Malcom. Both were pastors at First Presbyterian Church in Aurora, Illinois, and they brought a team of professional builders from their church in for three weeks to fix things up. It was a real-life extreme home makeover. We liked the results and were ready for guests.

Like in Mendenhall, we figured we would mostly reach out to black folks in the area, and we did. But the first people to come to our Samaritan Inn were a white, dirt-poor couple from out of town, whose vehicle had broken down and they had no other place to go.

In New Hebron, Mississippi, I grew up around poor whites who felt they were better than blacks and expected us to move out of their way when they were walking down the street. They experienced all of the advantages of being white. They were oppressors, and common knowledge through the years was that in rural areas, poor whites sought to become sheriffs, cops, or guards in order to have some power in society. So we did not have a great relationship with them. At the time I didn't realize these whites also had been damaged and that oppressing blacks gave them a sense of worth—a twisted sense of value, no doubt, but in their eyes, value nonetheless.

When our poor white guests arrived at the Samaritan Inn, I was caught off guard. I wanted to treat them like many people want to treat the poor: I was going to buy and prepare them food and even wash their dishes. Such acts of kindness would have made me feel good but also might have made them feel as if they couldn't think for themselves. Vera Mae had a better idea. She said, "Let's give them money and let them buy what they want to buy and eat what they want to eat."

On February 7, 1970, while I lay on the floor of the Simpson County Jail in Brandon, I made the decision to preach a gospel stronger than my racial identity and bigger than the segregation around me. It took this poor white couple coming into my home—and some good thinking by my wife—to teach me to start practicing what I was preaching.

To be honest, I had never given a second thought to poor whites. I still regarded them negatively—as redneck, trailer-park white trash. The wealthy white people could help me, but what good were the poor whites to me? But then that couple showed up on my doorstep. My automatic response was to treat them the way whites had treated poor blacks—to patronize them. But these people were teaching me, John Perkins, the guy who was supposed to be leading the church in reconciliation, a lesson in what it really means to be reconciled to one another.

—⚬⚬⚬—

Poor whites have lived in the backwoods and outskirts of towns throughout the South as long as there have been whites in the South. While the Southern gentlemen and belles of antebellum white society built a world of prosperous plantations, the first poor whites were likely descendants of Celtic criminals who had been banished to America. Poor whites included others too and were generally stereotyped as uneducated, lazy, simple outcasts. Early on they were labeled "poor white trash."

The term itself may have first been used in the Baltimore/Washington, DC, area to describe unskilled white laborers who competed with blacks for post–Civil War reconstruction jobs, but it soon made its way south and became an ugly slur, likely used interchangeably with *cracker*, *hillbilly*, and *redneck*.

Mark Twain, Harriet Beecher Stowe, and William Faulkner wrote about poor whites, but an English actress named Fanny Kemble gave the most disturbing account. On January 6, 1833, during a visit to the South, she wrote in her journal, "The slaves themselves entertain the very highest contempt for white servants, whom they designate as 'poor white trash.' It was equally used by whites."[1] Other accounts tell of times when blacks taunted by whites with racial slurs would fire back with the insult "poor white trash" as if it were tit for tat. Just how often the racial slurs flew, no one really knows, but none of it was good.

Just because some whites use heinous, callous, and abusive language to describe black people does not mean that we, as black people, are justified in responding with racial insults of our own. I can understand how it comes about. We as a people have been beaten down so much that calling poor whites a hurtful name is almost a cry for dignity. I get it. But it is a backward cry. In a way, it's an attempt to make poor whites feel the way we did when whites would fling racial slurs our way. But for us to do the same thing to poor whites that wealthy whites were doing to us only throws everyone into the same mud heap. A better way is possible. We all must have the compassion, wisdom, and mutual respect to rise above slander, slurs, and snubs to a place of love. What we ought to be striving for today is a new language of love and affirmation that will replace these hurtful slights. What if we started calling one another "friend," no matter our race, politics, or economic class? Friends, I like that.

—ᵚᵚ—

People often ask me if there's anything I would do differently if I could go back. Like anyone else, I'm aware of mistakes I've made, and I'm sure I could have done many things better. But there's one thing I know I would change if I had the chance to do it all over again: I would do more to help poor whites. I wish I could say that once my eyes were opened, my actions forever followed. But they did not.

I don't know if it's like this everywhere, but in Mississippi the relationship between blacks and poor whites has been complicated for as long as I can remember. Where I grew up, black and white sharecroppers living on the plantation got along with one another, at least somewhat. We would come together to slaughter a hog or help one another out from time to time. People knew one another and got along pretty well—as long as they were out in the countryside. However, as soon as some of those poor whites got into town, they would act like they despised the very same black folks they were neighbors with. One of these men—Old Henry, we called him—lived out near my grandma's house. He and his family were very poor. His sister and brothers and aunts all got along just fine with us, and so did Henry, when he was around home. But once he was dressed up and out on the town to shop, he became just as mean and racist as could be. Old Henry never did anything to physically harm anyone—he just didn't want the whites in town to think of him as being on the same level with us blacks.

The poor whites didn't really have anything going for them except their whiteness and the fact that blacks had to say "Yes, sir" and "No, sir" to them. Since that was about all they had, they held on to it real tight. That's why I developed a strong dislike of poor white folks for a while—they were the ones who did most of the damage to blacks in rural Mississippi. For example, the deputies who beat me in jail were poor whites. They had a little bit of authority and a black man to hate. I was one person who was lower than them in society, and they took out all their anger and fear and insecurity on me.

Many people in the black community weren't really any better though. I came from a family of bootleggers, who operated much like those who own a pawnshop today. Our customers were often the poor white folks trying to get some whiskey during Prohibition in Mississippi. It was a complicated situation, because we would give some credence to poor white folks to sell them liquor and get their money, but in reality, we resented them. Religious blacks also would pretend they liked the poor white folks but ultimately resented them too, telling jokes behind their backs and expressing hate for them. The truth is no one really liked the poor whites in Mississippi. They had almost no supporters, except the sheriffs, deputies, and Ku Klux Klan. The poor whites were even forced to have their own churches separate from the wealthy whites. While the wealthy whites went to First Baptist, First Methodist, or First Presbyterian in town, the poor whites were kept out, much like us black folks, and had their own country Pentecostal churches. This separation fed their resentment, and often the pastors of these churches were leaders in the Ku Klux Klan.

The wealthy whites also used the poor whites as tools of oppression, making them overseers or guards or sheriffs charged with taking care of the dirty work to keep black people in their place so they didn't have to. In reality, though, this just fueled the resentment between blacks and poor whites.

My daughter Joanie vividly remembers an experience she had during her first days at the all-white school:

> I got off the bus with a strong determined face. I went to my sixth-grade class and decided to sit in the front. There were two other blacks there—Patricia and Erskin—but they lasted only a few weeks before they returned to the black school. We looked at one another in shame and fear. Each day went by like a year. Playground time was the worst. One time, as I stood by the wall, not invited to play with the other children, a white girl stood by me against the wall. She was a trailer-park type and a bit of an outcast as well. We started talking. I felt she was different and would be my friend, but as soon as a group of popular girls came by, they looked at us in disdain and the white girl walked off. She told me later she couldn't be my friend. I guess she needed to survive the mean girls too. That was an awful blow to me. I didn't understand it then, but I understand it now. Trailer-park-poor whites in Mississippi needed to be accepted by the powers that be. Yes, they had more rights than blacks, but because they were poor, they had a lot of fitting in to do too.

You might remember in 2008 when then-presidential candidate Barack Obama said that poor white folks "cling to guns or religion." He was criticized for his politically incorrect comment and should not have made it, but he wasn't all wrong. For a long time, poor whites like Old Henry and the guards at the Simpson County Jail had a strategy for feeling better about themselves. Having blacks beneath them made them feel superior, but those old ways are rapidly going away. Thinking they were superior was wrong—don't think I'm saying it wasn't—but I've gotten to where I can feel compassion for them because something they had (or thought they had) is slipping away from them.

—⟋⟍—

In 1971, my friend Charles Evers ran for governor of Mississippi. His brother Medgar Evers was the state NAACP field secretary who was shot and killed in his driveway in 1963. Charles came pretty close to uniting blacks and poor whites around issues with which both could identify: pulpwood and poverty. His support of those working in the lumber industry persuaded poor whites to support him.

Charles didn't win the election, but he sure did an exceptional job of reaching across racial lines to try to uplift a downtrodden group of people.

—⟋⟍—

Until she passed away in early 2000, my cousin Teet and her husband, Hicks, lived out in the country. Sometimes, when I didn't have anything pressing on my schedule, I'd go down and spend the day with them. Their house and the countryside were a retreat for me. Sometimes we would visit the local church, which distributed food to people in need. While the food was from the government and food networks, this simple operation was run by black folks at the church who had been part of the civil rights movement and knew how to address needs in the community.

Not just blacks came for food. Many poor white folks came too. Sometimes when I visited the church, I would just hang back and watch the people come and go as they picked up food items. I always found the behavior of the white people quite curious. Their body language showed so much shame. One would almost think they were stealing the food.

I noted also that these white folks really didn't have a voice or anyone in power to stand up for them—that they too were victims exploited politically by those in power. Many times the man of the family would not even go inside to get the food; rather, he would sit outside in the truck and send in his wife. I wish that I had done more for this group of people. I've gone from almost hating them (when I was young and angry and they were bigoted and violent) to genuinely loving them as brothers and sisters. I think about how many poor whites respond to me so positively when I speak today. Often I can see a spark in their eyes. I'm truly sorry that I've neglected the needs of these neighbors of mine and have not responded often enough to the spark.

4

Fighting without Fists

Joe Louis was one of our heroes: a famous black man who knew how to fight with his fists. Louis, born the son of a sharecropper from Alabama, was called the "Brown Bomber." When I was a kid, for blacks he was our Jim Thorpe, our Jackie Robinson, our LeBron James, our Stephen Curry, our Babe Ruth. He was the best heavyweight boxer in the world.

In those days I couldn't watch boxing matches or any sports on television—we had no ESPN, no internet, not even a Motorola TV set with rabbit ears. My family didn't even possess a radio. But Mr. Fred Bush had one. Mr. Bush was the white owner of the plantation where we lived as sharecroppers at the time. He always encouraged me, just as he did his own children.

I remember the day as if it were yesterday. On June 22, 1938, six days after my eighth birthday, my uncle, my brother, and I scampered up to the Bush house to join others listening to the radio broadcast of the battle of the century. Joe Louis was pitted in a rematch against the only man who had ever defeated him—Germany's Max Schmeling. The three of us had to stay on the porch and listen from a slight distance, but the Bushes made sure the radio volume was turned up so we could hear. At that time it was a big deal that a plantation owner would allow us to be even that close.

Louis opened with two powerful left hooks, and Schmeling was hobbled. The 70,000 fans at the old Yankee Stadium in New York where the fight was taking place roared in approval, and so did we, trying not to make too much noise. Schmeling threw only two punches the entire bout, and Louis knocked him down three times. Thump. Thump. Thump. The last jab ended the fight, which had lasted only two minutes and four seconds. I was jubilant!

As blacks, we celebrated the Brown Bomber's triumph—so did all of America. President Franklin Roosevelt even invited Louis to the White House, where the president jokingly squeezed the boxer's biceps. It was a big win.

The Louis-Schmeling fights had muddy racial overtones, made even more complex with the outbreak of World War II a year after Louis's win. Schmeling was a German paratrooper and had unwittingly become a symbol of Aryan superiority for some, even appearing in a rally with Adolf Hitler. However, the German boxer was not a member of the Nazi Party, and it was later learned that he had risked his life to save two Jewish children. Of course, as an eight-year-old boy, I knew none of this. All I knew was that one of us, a black *and* an American, was the boxing champion of the world.

—⟋⟋⟍—

Outside the boxing ring, I have a very different take on fighting.

The first clash I witnessed in real life took place a little more than a year before we huddled on the Bushes' porch to listen to the battle of the century. I was six years old and probably helping Grandma with the chores on a nice Saturday afternoon. Uncle Bud burst into the house, all sweaty with rage. He had been gambling with some friends, not far from the house, and they had caught one of the players cheating. The trickster deserved to be shot! Uncle Bud grabbed his gun and stormed outside, intent on doing "justice" with a bullet.

Grandma was scared and would have none of that. She knew the outcome would not be good or just for anyone. After catching up with Uncle Bud in the yard, Grandma tried to wrestle the loaded weapon away from him. I was scared. Here was a mother fighting with her son who desperately wanted to kill another man. Finally, thankfully, she got the gun away from him.

Though I was only a kid, the fight left a strong impression on me. I didn't like the fear, ugliness, and futility of it all. What good would have come if my Uncle Bud had shot the cheating gambler? He would have felt a rush for a moment and then landed in jail—or worse. And what if the gun had gone off while he was struggling with my grandma? I still shudder to this day when I think about it.

Another time, not too long after that, some teenage boys came to our house to get some whiskey. My aunt's boyfriend, Dudley Longeno, was a little intoxicated but not quite drunk (they called it "high" in those days), and he was clowning around with his friends when they started beating him up. He was cursing and striking back but was not in any shape to land many blows.

That time there was no gun, but it was a big brawl—even my aunt was screaming and throwing fists. I was only seven years old, but I pushed my way right into the middle of the fracas and attempted to stop it. There was something corrective in me even back then, and I didn't want to see anyone hurt. I've always known it's important to not take advantage of people, even someone under the influence of whiskey. Everyone was surprised when I stepped in to defend Dudley. If they were going to beat up my aunt's boyfriend, they were going to have to beat up me too. So they all stopped fighting.

—⚬—

I never intentionally set out to be a peacemaker, but through the years I have come face-to-face with quite a number of fights, and each time, something would rise inside me that was stronger than the present danger or fear.

One time I was in Harlem and saw a man beating a woman; it looked like he was going to kill her. This was happening near a church on a Sunday, and a number of people were standing around outside, just watching or trying to ignore what was going on. I told everyone around we needed to do something, but they were afraid to get involved.

I should have been fearful too, but something got into me. I walked up to the man, who was in a total rage, and told him, "Don't do that. You're killing her. It's not worth it." He stopped. It was almost like when Jesus calmed the storm at sea—it got that quiet and still. Whew, was I surprised! So were the others who were watching. They told me later how dangerous it was to have stopped the man because they knew him and were certain he was going to turn on me too.

I don't set out to do these things—they just happen. Another time, while I was visiting Nairobi, Kenya, I saw a woman running away from a man who was beating her. The custom among some Kenyans gives a man the prerogative to beat "his woman." Thankfully, I didn't know that until afterward. When I said I was going to step in, the people I was with were terrified; they feared for my life. But I could not just stand there. I knew what it was like to be beaten by someone who had absolute authority over me—someone who could beat me for any reason he wanted, or for no reason at all. I stepped between the man and the woman. The man was shocked. He did not touch me or say a word. He just walked away. Of course, I have no idea what happened later, but at least on that day the beating stopped.

—⚏—

Injustice is an evil in society that must be fought. But what does that fight look like? The word *fight* immediately makes most people think of violence—it conjures images of fisticuffs and physical domination. But other ways to combat the wrongs in society do exist. In 1955, on the eve of the December 5 bus boycott in Montgomery, Alabama, Dr. King put it this way:

> Now let us say that we are not here advocating violence. We have overcome that. I want it to be known throughout Montgomery and throughout this nation that we are Christian people. We believe in the Christian religion. We believe in the teachings of Jesus. The only weapon that we have in our hands this evening is the weapon of protest.[1]

One of the great surprises of recent history is this idea of nonviolent protest. Dr. King, Gandhi, Cesar Chavez, Bishop Desmond Tutu, Nelson Mandela (after he came out of prison), and others led revolutions that didn't depend on bloodshed and the violent overthrow of power structures. They realized the power in what Jesus taught about loving our enemies.

In the face of power, some resort to violence as a way to create chaos. That's terrorism. That's what people use when they don't have the power to win. Nonviolence is a better way. It's radical. And the hope is that it's so different that the enemy, seeing your nonviolent actions, will not be violent toward you. This idea dominated the civil rights movement.

Of course, one of the challenges Martin Luther King Jr., Mahatma Gandhi, and other leaders faced was keeping their followers convinced that love is a better way to fight than violence. So they found unique ways. Gandhi and Cesar Chavez, for example, were great fasters and used that to their advantage. Their hunger strikes had multiple goals. For instance, Chavez used fasting as a way to restrain his union workers when they would start to get violent. He didn't want them to kill people, but the situation was out of his control. So he would fast.

Back in Mendenhall, I had my own difficulty helping people understand love is a better way to fight than violence. As the young people in the area woke up to the civil rights movement, I started getting frequent reports of broken windows at local businesses or vandalized washing machines at the laundromat. Soon I found out that my sons were involved in these destructive activities. They saw such acts as an extension of the movement. So then I was really in a mess. Everybody knew this vandalism was connected to the civil rights movement, and I was one of the leaders of that movement in our community. I knew people would think I was condoning violent behavior, which I certainly didn't. Consequently, I had some serious conversations with my kids and others in the community to let them know, like Dr. King said, they shouldn't be like the enemy, fighting fire with fire. I also did some fasting and praying. Like Chavez, I had a situation I desperately wanted to change but couldn't really control on my own. I quickly came to understand that nonviolence takes more strength than violence—and it takes more than just human strength. It takes God's strength working in human beings to produce self-control, gentleness, and the other fruit of the Holy Spirit. God's power comes in our weakness and brokenness.

Some whites at the time, I'm told, were afraid that blacks—as we gained rights and power, and as our population grew—would take over the country. Some also feared that blacks would then kill the whites who had been oppressing them. Although I've just acknowledged the potential for violent behavior by those who have been oppressed, I believe this particular fear is unfounded. The sad truth is that when black anger against racism boils over, the black community usually suffers the most damage. I think most blacks who riot would say they're rioting in reaction to some white act of violence or injustice—like after the Rodney King verdict. People were angry and disappointed. They felt that whites who still wanted to keep blacks oppressed had taken care of these white officers and gotten them out of jail. Now, in the riots that followed the verdict, some black rioters did pull one white man from his truck and beat him. But most of the hostile energy turned toward damaging property within the black community—and carrying off televisions and other loot.

More recently, the same type of violence occurred in the wake of the deaths of Michael Brown in Ferguson, Missouri, and Eric Garner in New York City. Both men were black and died at the hands of white police officers. The anger from both blacks and whites concerning these deaths was intense, and people were unable to listen to one another. Many whites thought the violence and rioting were unnecessary, but many blacks said that in the wake of so much oppression, they didn't know how else to respond.

These differing reactions resulted from our own polarization and victimization in the African American community. Whites need to take some responsibility for centuries of imperialism and failing to repent, but blacks also need to take some responsibility for the breakdown of our families. We all need to take responsibility for providing equal education and job training for all people and doing a better job of training our police officers not to resort to brutality. The nonviolent Black Lives Matter activist movement has been a successful and much-needed way to bring attention to the problem of violence against black people. But what about the epidemic of violence within our own African American community—African Americans killing one another? That too needs to be addressed. We the church are called to be the light that shines in these dark places.

But even more, the church needs to be a witness to the world of what nonviolent change can look like. We should be leading the way in offering alternatives to the broken systems of this world, so that cycles of poverty and hatred don't lead to violent reactions. Whatever the solution, the church must work it out together.

People are quick to find something or someone to blame in these situations. For example, many criticize the state of America's poor, urban schools and place the blame on teachers or curriculums that don't teach the students how to grow up and be successful. They condemn the government for not giving schools enough funding or attack parents who choose to send their children to private or Christian schools, leaving the poor behind. Some of these arguments might be valid, but the issue is bigger than this. It's more than education or any other single issue.

One of the tenets of CCDA is holistic development, or looking for a multifaceted approach to caring and ministering to others. When we try to pin these issues on a single problem, we are more likely to resort to violence. We think that by violently eliminating one thing, we can solve the entire issue. But when we recognize that incidents like the Michael Brown case are the result of many different broken systems, we realize that violence won't solve anything. Instead, we need to talk to one another, listen to one another, be willing to confess our sins to one another and, in turn, forgive one another. When we have these types of conversations, we begin to understand where the roots of some of the problems lie.

American society has lost its capacity for pluralism in many ways. We have begun to believe that if others don't agree with us, then we don't have to listen to them. We dehumanize people who don't think like we do and, consequently, justify our violence against them. But we all are created in God's image. We all are His children. We live in a country that proclaims freedom of speech and freedom of expression, and we must be willing to listen to and try to understand the thoughts and ideas of others. This is the way to make change happen without violence.

—⁂—

The apostle Paul, before his conversion, knew all about fighting. He condoned extreme violence—and maybe even participated in it. After his encounter with Jesus, though, he became the kind of man who would endure violence at the hands of others without returning blow for blow. When Paul wrote to his disciple Timothy,

"I have fought the good fight" (2 Tim. 4:7 NKJV), he was not referring to anything he had accomplished with his fists. My prayer is that as I approach the end of my days, I too will be able to say that I have come to understand what the "good fight" is and that I have persevered in that battle.

5

The Three Rs

Sometime around 1825, a British man named Sir William Curtis coined the phrase "the three Rs." Like most people today, he meant Reading, wRiting and aRithmetic. He had to stretch a little to actually nail the three Rs, but it worked.

My teachers probably stressed these Rs as the fundamentals of education, but when I was a child they never really stuck. Reading wasn't on my to-do list until Uncle Bud signed up our family to receive the daily newspaper just before and during World War II. That's when I discovered comic strips! I still smile when I think about Popeye, Dagwood Bumstead, and Sky King. And I don't have to stretch too far to see how Jiggs and Maggie (the characters in the strip *Bringing Up Father*) helped shape my own worldview and dreams. Jiggs was a working-class Irish immigrant who had struck it rich but still struggled with his anxieties, bugaboos, and aspirations. Sometimes I see a smidgen of Jiggs in myself. I have what the world would call success—at least a measure of it—but I still struggle with that boy inside me, the one raised in the backwoods of Mississippi.

I don't think Uncle Bud realized the contribution he was making to my life by subscribing to a daily newspaper, but the older I get, the more I recognize how much that newspaper did for me. I would look at the news articles too, eventually making it a habit. To this day I prefer to read the news and digest it rather than hear TV commentators and their spin.

During the early days in Mendenhall, a group of us developed and focused on a different set of three Rs: relocation, reconciliation, and redistribution. The group included Artis Fletcher, Dolphus Weary, H. Spees, and me. We identified and defined these three Rs, but my family and friends had been living them out since relocating from California back to Mississippi.

We had programs and looked at statistics. H. even wrote an impressive paper. Yet for me, real community development has always flowed from an awareness of what it means to be a good neighbor and then living out that knowledge. Good neighbors go beyond caring for others—they strengthen them as well. When individuals grow, families grow. When families grow, communities grow. When we live out the three Rs, community development happens. And that's what we tried to do during that time—every day, no matter our neighborhood, from Mendenhall to Jackson to Pasadena and back to Jackson and around the world. Those three Rs will work worldwide.

—⚍—

The first R is the toughest but most crucial one. People jump on the relocation bandwagon with enthusiasm, then want to compromise when they actually try to live it out. To relocate means to move from one place to another, from the old to the new. It can be exciting, profoundly biblical, and even romantic in an odd way.

Jesus modeled relocation. He is the one who "became flesh and dwelt among us" (John 1:14 NKJV). Put simply, relocation means living in the community where God has called you. But relocation consists of much more than changing your zip code. Living out the first R means becoming involved in the community, knowing your neighbors, and being aware of the issues that confront them on a daily basis. It goes even further. Once you know their hurts and feel their pain, your neighbors' issues become yours too.

People often say they need to be a voice *for* the voiceless, which sounds good but often ends up becoming imperialistic and patronizing. The oppressed already have a voice; the problem is that no one is listening. I am talking about allowing their voice to be heard. The more privileged people in society need to hear the voice of the oppressed and marginalized. We are here not to talk for them but, rather, to listen to them and provide avenues for people outside of the community to hear them as well. We can lament the pain of others and do a few things to alleviate it from afar. We can visit the rough ghettos and homeless shelters. That is good and needed, but we cross a threshold to a deeper place when we go from simply being visitors and guests to living as neighbors and family.

To me, relocation is about incarnation. The ancient Chinese philosopher Lau Tzu provided a good description of what this means: "Go to the people. Live with them. Learn from them. Love them. Start with what they know. Build with what they have. But with the best leaders when the work is done, the task accomplished, the people will say 'We have done this ourselves.'"[1] When we live in a community together, we get to know one another. Sometimes getting to know our neighbors is hard because we may have disagreements or fall victim to the same problems that they face—crime, substandard schools, declining property values, and so on. In the case of crime, it may even be some of our neighbors who victimize us. For instance, personally, not long ago someone in our community stole Vera Mae's car. She can't drive it anymore, but the theft was still wrong, and we were still hurt that someone did that to us.

But oftentimes the close connection gained from living as neighbors and family brings joy—we discover one another's gifts and strengths we might never have noticed from a distance. With low-income communities especially, it's much easier to see the positive things from the inside. When you're outside looking in—or if you just drive through from time to time—you're more likely to see only the problems and needs. Relocation is an equalizer. It helps people overcome alienation and fosters vibrant, close relationships. Family.

Let's dig into this a little deeper. But first let me offer a word of caution. Check your motivation before calling U-Haul. If you move to the inner city (or another low-income community) solely out of guilt or for the thrill of it, it almost never works out. You will swoop in with big dreams and quickly be flattened by reality. Things will happen—and few of them will be what you expected. People will disappoint and hurt you. Funds will run low. And a neighborhood kid may break into your car! I've seen a lot of people come and go. Now, some of those people moved on because God called them somewhere else, and they have continued to live out these principles in their new locations or have adapted them according to where God has called them. That's good. But others left because their expectations weren't met, or because it got too painful, and they retreated to whatever was familiar and comfortable to them.

My observation, in general, has been that some of the individuals and families who started with flawed motivations ended up being the most broken. While I must be careful not to judge and certainly do not know every circumstance, I wonder whether some were listening to their own hearts rather than God's voice.

No formula exists to figure out where you should go to best serve God. You can only listen to His voice. If He calls you to a struggling community, then you must accept that life's going to be tough. You must stick to your commitment and, in the end, realize that as much as you are serving others, ultimately you are serving God.

Also, approach relocation with humility. You cannot move into a neighborhood thinking that your presence or kindness is going to change the whole neighborhood or every person you come into contact with. The truth is people will deceive you wherever you go. Some folks I have worked with for years have learned all the language around relocation and the three Rs but use that language to exploit rather than build a deeper relationship with Jesus Christ. They know how to use a person's kindness and goodwill to get what they want, but in the end, they don't want real conversion or to grow in the body of Christ. It's a hard truth, but if you really want to help people in a way that encourages growth rather than dependency, you have to be aware of this truth.

Sometimes I think we have lost the concept of the benefit of sacrifice in Christianity. We underestimate how God uses hard times and self-denial to make us stronger. Many people, when they find out that I choose to live in West Jackson, either write me off as crazy or want to make me into some kind of martyr. I am neither.

When you go to the place God has called you to go, are you a martyr or are you living out the highest possible calling in your life? Do you really lose anything when you give up everything to get exactly what God wants for you?

—ɰ—

God calls some people to leave one place and go to another, where they live out their lives. At other times, the move is temporary, but in God's timing. Toward the end of my first tenure in Jackson, my work had expanded to a national, even an international, level. My passion was to expand the Christian community development movement to cities everywhere.

The late Al Whittaker, a friend, was on my ministry board at the time. He confirmed my thoughts and told me, "With the work you seem called to do, it doesn't matter what city you live in." I had completed my part of the task in Jackson, and it was time to move on.

Another board member, Donna Lake, made it even easier. Donna and her husband, Dr. Kevin Lake, had an empty guesthouse in Pasadena, California, and invited Vera Mae and me to stay as long as we needed to get clear direction on our next move. We drove from Jackson to Pasadena, stopping to visit friends in Dallas and Albuquerque along the way. I was flying high, feeling free and joyous. While I loved every minute of living and working in Mississippi, and

I loved the people there, I knew I was on to my next assignment. Vera Mae? She left behind the children she was teaching in what we called the Good News Club, and I knew she would miss them. But I didn't realize how much. I think we were about twenty miles outside of Jackson when I glanced over to her and saw the tears in her eyes. She is not one to complain when she knows God is leading, but as she reminisced, the tears flowed.

While I like to meditate on God's Word and listen for His voice, I am not one to sit for days on end. Almost as soon as we arrived in California, I was visiting people and listening to them talk about their struggles. Drugs. Joblessness. Broken families. Crime. Gangs. The stories about the troubles growing in northwest Pasadena really got to me.

Vera Mae was out and about too. She visited a church with a friend and liked the pastor's preaching. I listened to some cassette tapes of his sermons and liked what I heard. We wanted to live in the community that surrounded whichever church we decided to attend. After all, how else would we become part of the community? So that's how we came to buy a house on the most dangerous street corner in Pasadena.

We drove out to a particular house that was for sale, but it was too run down, and Vera Mae just shook her head no. The house across the street, however, was also for sale and in better shape—not much but enough so that Vera Mae would consider it. A ninety-four-year-old woman owned and lived in the house. We didn't have quite enough for the down payment—even then houses were more expensive in California than in Mississippi—so we were nervous that she would not want to sell to us, but she did. Later we learned that the house had been on the market for two years and the woman was afraid we would see all the drug dealers on the street and be scared off. Little did she know what would come about in the future.

Once we bought the house, there was no going back to Jackson. We started Bible studies, prayer meetings, Good News Clubs, and everything we do. But the idea of relocation cannot be just about outsiders coming in; it has to be centered on leaders being raised up from within. I remember telling Vera Mae one night that the only way we could make change happen was if we instilled in these children a love for their community that was stronger than the desire to get out. As more and more people with resources move out, the neighborhoods become poorer and poorer, and the community becomes drained of its most valuable asset. One of my best friends, Wayne Gordon, always said that the Remainers, those who stay behind, are the glue that holds a community together and helps make it a better place to live.

—m—

The second R—reconciliation—is the heart of the gospel. It is the process by which God brings us to Him and keeps us. It is the main activating force within the redemptive idea. It is the process of forgiveness of sin. The Bible makes it clear that "God was in Christ reconciling the world to Himself" (2 Cor. 5:19 NKJV). It's also the process by which believers in Christ are joined to one another: "His purpose was to create in himself one new humanity out of the two, thus making peace, and in one body to reconcile both of them to God through the cross, by which he put to death their hostility" (Eph. 2:15–16). He's working out our forgiveness. It's His intention to hold us together through reconciliation. Reconciliation is working in the process of forgiveness—being forgiven and forgiving others. It's an ongoing, living thing in the Bible. It's active. It's a moving force. We work out the idea of redemption with redemptive living. Our churches today make reconciliation an event or an institution, rather than treating it as a gift from God and an integral part of the gospel message in general.

Paul understood the importance of reconciliation. We read in Galatians the account of how Peter withdrew from fellowship with gentile believers—and how Paul confronted him:

Now when Peter had come to Antioch, I withstood him to his face, because he was to be blamed; for before certain men came from James, he would eat with the Gentiles; but when they came, he withdrew and separated himself, fearing those who were of the circumcision. And the rest of the Jews also played the hypocrite with him, so that even Barnabas was carried away with their hypocrisy.

But when I saw that they were not straightforward about the truth of the gospel, I said to Peter before them all, "If you, being a Jew, live in the manner of Gentiles and not as the Jews, why do you compel Gentiles to live as Jews? . . . A man is not justified by the works of the law but by faith in Jesus Christ, even we have believed in Christ Jesus, that we might be justified by faith in Christ and not by the works of the law; for by the works of the law no flesh shall be justified." (2:11–16 NKJV)

The way Peter allowed ethnicity to divide the early church and tried to impose his own cultural values on fellow Christians was not in line with the truth of the gospel. Paul was making a serious charge! Clearly, God desires reconciliation between believers with different ethnic backgrounds. The way we accommodate racism and bigotry in the church, even today, is a heresy and a major blind spot.

But even if our gospel is veiled, it is veiled to those who are perishing, whose minds the god of this age has blinded, who do not believe, lest the light of the gospel of the glory of Christ, who is the image of God, should shine on them. For we do not preach ourselves, but Christ Jesus the Lord, and ourselves your bondservants for Jesus' sake. For it is the God who commanded light to shine out of darkness, who has shone in our hearts to give the light of the knowledge of the glory of God in the face of Jesus Christ. (2 Cor. 4:3–6 NKJV)

When I first started preaching that message in the 1960s, I met huge resistance from many churches. Today, many Christians embrace the idea of reconciliation, and that encourages me. I fear sometimes, though, that our vision is still too small.

God is all about reconciliation, but we run the risk of missing Him when we allow racial reconciliation, or any kind of reconciliation, to rise as the dominating force—if we allow it rather than God Himself to become the ultimate goal. I see how this happens—it makes sense when we have been so damaged by division, hostility, and oppression. But some of the ways we go about fiddling with our relationships with one another in the name of reconciliation reveal the extent of our own damage—sometimes even of our own obsession with race. We spend too much time trying to fix the things we don't like rather than simply reconciling everything to God. Instead, reconciliation is most successful when churches treat it not as a project or an event but as a way of life. It simply becomes the congregation's commitment to evangelism and discipleship—it's how they fulfill the Great Commission. Things only get fixed—truly fixed—when they are mended by God through faith. Often we have it backward, trying to fix things for God rather than letting God fix things through us.

My family and I returned to Jackson in 1996, after living in Pasadena for fifteen years. A couple of my kids and grandkids attend Redeemer Presbyterian Church in Jackson. Let me give you a little history about this church. Before Redeemer existed, a congregation called Trinity Presbyterian Church held services in Redeemer's current location. Trinity, a predominantly white congregation, has had a long-standing relationship with New Horizon, the predominantly black charismatic church I currently attend in Jackson. Trinity and New Horizon have come together for mission work and other outreach efforts, which I consider very important to reconciliation. Building relationships across racial lines for the sake of bringing the gospel message to people who haven't heard it is a beautiful picture of what I believe God wants for His church.

The neighborhood around Trinity started to change a few years ago. It had been mostly white but was becoming mostly black. The church was having trouble growing, and a building became available in a different area of town that would give the congregation room to expand. The neighborhood would also be more conducive to growth in terms of white members. Trinity's members and board discussed at length what to do. Eventually they decided to move, but a number of members—white members—didn't want to go. Some of the women were meeting for a Bible study with Vera Mae and working with neighborhood kids after school. This was their community. So Trinity "planted" Redeemer in the original location.

It pains me any time I see a church move out of a community with race as a contributing factor. Too often when this happens, a white congregation leaves behind an empty building in a dying neighborhood rather than choosing a creative solution or simply staying on course. So the Trinity and Redeemer story isn't flawless, but I am encouraged by the outcome.

Today, Redeemer's congregation is about 45 percent black, but even in the beginning, when a much higher percentage of whites attended, the church brought in Michael Campbell, a black man from Miami, to be the senior pastor. To see a majority-white congregation choose a black leader is significant. And the congregation's membership is growing—whites, blacks, and a few Asians too. Campbell's position is somewhat unique, because it is much less common to see blacks leading mostly white congregations.

On the one hand, whites need to recognize and affirm the many gifts, including the gift of leadership, that blacks bring to the table. At the same time, I long to see black pastors reaching out, breaking down walls, and seeking a multiethnic church body.

Of course, reconciliation isn't just about being in relationship with people from different backgrounds. It's about mending broken relationships through repentance and forgiveness. Sometimes the repentance and forgiveness are on behalf of whole groups of people.

In 2008, I traveled to Glendale, California, to participate in a conference sponsored by seven local Chinese churches. I preached on a Friday night, a Saturday night, and a Sunday morning. Those attending the conference had come together for three days to talk about reconciliation. During one presentation, I was given my honorarium check. The pastor making the presentation used part of his time to apologize to me. He talked about how Chinese people used to buy property with deeds that specified "no blacks allowed." They had accepted that racist clause even though they also had benefited from changes that blacks had fought for during the civil rights movement.

One leader described how during the civil rights movement many Chinese had gotten rich while blacks had fought for them to have equal rights and not be discriminated against. That's powerful insight. He basically said, "We got rich and never did anything. This is our opportunity to ask for forgiveness and say thank you." To be thankful and ask for forgiveness is true reconciliation. The honorarium check represented an atonement—bringing forth something that is meaningful. We weren't just shaking hands and eating and drinking tea together—our relationship had become more than that.

This brother was repenting on behalf of his people for the wrongs that had been done to my people. It was a little overwhelming to go up there and accept the apology, but I did. After the service, a long line of people stopped me to confess their own prejudice and feelings of guilt. It was an extremely humbling experience.

Later when I talked more with the Chinese church leaders, they had more to say about the need for Chinese Christians to repent and be reconciled. They explained the problem: they were too Chinese-focused. Most of the time when they talked about planting a church, they envisioned a Chinese church. When they went out to eat, they ate at a Chinese restaurant. Everything was Chinese. They wanted to change and were planting a multicultural church. They brought me out to California to share the biblical texts as well as my own experiences and convictions that had shaped my thoughts on planting multicultural churches.

Now, I have traveled to places like New Zealand, Australia, China, Jamaica, Malaysia, Brazil, and all over Africa trying to spread this vision of Christian community development and the biblical truth of reconciliation. The vision for true reconciliation is on the rise all over the world. It's like what John saw in Revelation—people from every nation coming to God's kingdom where His redemptive story is approaching its eternal state. If God is in it, it's going to happen. And we know that God is in it, so it *is* going to happen. There is no turning back.

—⚏—

Because reconciliation is so hard to live out on a consistent basis, I fully believe that it's one of the greatest displays of God's redemptive power. Our world is aflame with racial, tribal, and other kinds of tensions between groups of people. We have taken God's definition of reconciliation and made room for bigotry by inserting race into the concept. Racial reconciliation is not a biblical term. People use race as a slave master, a means of injustice and exploitation. The very purpose of the gospel is to reconcile human beings to God and to one another. When human beings are reconciled to God, their relationship with every culture is in harmony. A reconciled church would be an incredible testimony to God's ability to do things that are impossible for human beings to accomplish on their own. So what I call for—what I believe the gospel calls for—is unity across ethnic and cultural barriers. Jesus prayed for that the night before He died: "That [all believers] may be brought to complete unity. Then the world will know that you sent me and have loved them even as you have loved me" (John 17:23). Our unity—our reconciliation—bears witness to the world of the surpassing love of God in Jesus Christ.

—⚏—

The third R—redistribution—tends to make some folks nervous. They hear the word and think it's some sort of Robin Hood thing or a Communist conspiracy—taking from the rich and giving to the poor. That's not what I mean at all. That wouldn't work anyway.

I'm not suggesting that we move money around or level everything out so everyone has exactly the same amount.

What I envision is Christians developing a new perspective on resources. Look around at everything God has created in this world! How can there not be enough to meet everyone's basic needs—food, housing, clothing, health care, and so on? We ought to talk about redistributing opportunities. Too much free stuff undermines people's dignity and feelings of value. The value is more appreciated when it comes out of one's own effort. In the Bible, the book of Ruth demonstrates the principle of redistribution quite well. When we talk about redistribution, we're really talking about stewardship. The problem, of course, is that we've gotten away from the understanding that all of the resources belong to God, and that we are stewards of whatever portion of those resources He has entrusted to us.

Unfortunately, America's current welfare system creates dependency and entitlement. Homeless shelters and food pantries are doing a good job helping people, but their scope isn't large enough, and they don't offer training for jobs or ways to connect people to work. What I would like to see is a new alternative. It's estimated that 1 percent of the people in the world own 50 percent of the world's wealth.[2] Again, I'm not asking these billionaires to just give their money away to every person on the street but, rather, to help create an alternative system. These billionaires have the resources and businesses to provide job opportunities and fund nonprofits that can offer training schools for those who have never worked before. This is real redistribution: the people with the most skills and opportunities sharing with those who don't have them.

Take, for example, a friend of mine who owns a car dealership and has provided for me and my ministry with his resources in so many ways. One time he went with me to an event in San Diego for Plant with Purpose (formerly Floresta), an organization that works in rural areas all over the world developing local leaders and providing sustainable agriculture and land restoration training, savings-led microfinance, and church mobilization. When my friend learned about all this organization does, he became actively involved and even served on its board of directors. Plant with Purpose is a wonderful example of how to properly implement redistribution.

Many of the people I see in the community around me have been damaged by broken families and the poor school systems that don't have the money or committed teachers to help train the children coming up. This is a large-scale problem. Consequently, the church needs to come alongside the business community to provide moral training and familial love that affirms the dignity of these children. The church can care well for these kids—but it cannot do it alone. This is why the schools are integral to these conversations as well. Redistribution requires a holistic approach. Yes, it has to do with economics, but it also has to do with the resources and opportunities people have access to that help them grow and flourish. The resources to make this happen do exist—there is plenty to go around—the question is how do we reach the church, the business community, the government, the schools, and all who have an interest in organizing a type of redistribution that truly empowers people?

The early church gives us an example of what redistribution looks like:

> All the believers were one in heart and mind. No one claimed that any of their possessions was their own, but they shared everything they had. With great power the apostles continued to testify to the resurrection of the Lord Jesus. And God's grace was so powerfully at work in them all that there were no needy persons among them. For from time to time those who owned land or houses sold them, brought the money from the sales and put it at the apostles' feet, and it was distributed to anyone who had need. (Acts 4:32–35)

Apparently God placed enough wealth within the community of believers to meet the needs of the whole community—as long as those who had a greater share of the wealth remained willing to give some part of what they had for the benefit of others. While this is a wonderful model that ought to be lived out among believers, it is unique in the sense that these people were there from every nation under heaven and had given themselves to God. The joy they experienced was so complete, and their giving was completely out of a sense of joy. It is a model that came out of the joy, respect, and love they had for one another.

In today's society, examples of redistribution can also be found. For instance, let's look at the University Presbyterian Church on the University of Washington campus. Housing is a big need for many students. So some wealthy businesspeople have sold their large homes, moved into smaller homes in the community where the college is located, and bought additional houses in the area to use for student housing.

Another program that is somewhat of a spin-off of the same group involves businesspeople buying large plots of land in Latin America, breaking the land up into smaller plots, and providing ownership opportunities to people there who have never owned land before. What they're discovering is that having smaller pieces of land owned by a larger number of people is making the society as a whole more productive. I guess it shouldn't be surprising that God's way of doing things is the best way!

Habitat for Humanity is one of the most effective Christian organizations involved in redistribution efforts. People put some sweat equity into building their home and also have to pay some money back to Habitat for the project, but without any interest. This allows low-income families the opportunity to own their own home.

Programs like this instill gratitude in people and help them see the value of ownership, caring for and respecting the things they own. When people have ownership over something, if they help pay for it or build it, they are much more likely to take care of it than if it is just handed to them for free.

—∿—

Something I've learned about these three Rs over the years is that if you get one or two of them, the others tend to follow, though really none are easy. I believe that's because they're all tied to the idea of loving God and loving our neighbors. Relocation is imitating Christ, who "made himself nothing by taking the very nature of a servant, being made in human likeness" (Phil. 2:7) so He could show us the full extent of God's love. Reconciliation is God bringing people into relationship with Himself and other people. Redistribution is caring for others' needs as we care for our own.

If we're committed to these central values, we're eventually going to see all of their manifestations in our lives. It's like the fruit of the Spirit. You don't just pick one and grow it. As the Spirit works on your character, all of these aspects of God's character begin to be revealed in you: "love, joy, peace, longsuffering, kindness, goodness, faithfulness, gentleness, self-control" (Gal. 5:22–23 NKJV).

In the same way, if you're living in a community of need (relocation), and you're developing deep relationships with your neighbors (reconciliation), you're going to start looking for how the resources you have access to can benefit these neighbors you love (redistribution), and it's joyful. If you don't want to do it, don't do it. Do it cheerfully. I'm not talking about some system. I'm not talking about socialism or capitalism. These are people who want to be social or people who have capital and want to be good stewards and invest their resources in a way that has the best eternal return, for the highest dividend we can receive is discipleship that leads to Christian character development. I'm not talking about selfishness—keep your money, your misery, your fear, your suspicion. The poor don't need any more of that. Or, if you're in the community (relocation) and investing your resources in ways that improve life for your neighbors (redistribution), you're likely to develop significant relationships as you work side by side with people who come from different backgrounds (reconciliation).

Of course, to live out these principles day to day, we need to be intentional. But I really do believe that as we practice each of them, they all become more a part of our fundamental approach to life, and we become better able to love our neighbors as ourselves. Maybe this is exactly what Jesus had in mind when He told us to go into the world, making disciples of every nation.

6

Incarnation
(Being Jesus in the Flesh)

For God, who said, "Let light shine out of darkness," made his light shine in our hearts to give us the light of the knowledge of God's glory displayed in the face of Christ.

—2 Corinthians 4:6

My thinking about the principle of relocation began because of a practical need: I was trying to raise up indigenous leaders in Mendenhall. My hope for the young people I was working with was that they would go off and get some education—something many Mississippians before them had done—and then return to our community and use what they had learned to benefit others—something few Mississippians before them had done.

This returning part was the harder sell. Once people escaped Mississippi's crushing poverty and racism, they didn't generally want to come back. I was delighted when God worked in the hearts of several of our young people to do just what I'd hoped. Dolphus and Rosie Weary, Artis and Carolyn Fletcher, and others studied in California and Washington, DC, and then returned to Mendenhall to devote decades ministering in the community.

Pretty soon my thinking expanded, and I started talking about people coming from outside the community to make their homes with us and join in the work. We started "indigenizing" people, as I call it. They might not have grown up in the community, but they made it their home in meaningful ways—buying houses, joining neighborhood associations, raising kids, starting businesses, and loving their neighbors.

Eventually, I realized that this strategy of indigenizing, which I'd stumbled into almost by accident, had some similarities to one of the great mysteries of the Bible—the incarnation of God in the person of Jesus. John began his Gospel with this amazing account: "In the beginning was the Word, and the Word was with God, and the Word was God. He was with God in the beginning. . . . The Word became flesh and made his dwelling among us. We have seen his glory, the glory of the one and only Son, who came from the Father, full of grace and truth" (John 1:1–2, 14). It took me a while to wrestle with this great mystery of God, the creator of all things, taking on the form of one of His creations. Paul pondered the incarnation too: "And without controversy great is the mystery of godliness: God was manifested in the flesh, justified in the Spirit, seen by angels, preached among the Gentiles, believed on in the world, received up in glory" (1 Tim. 3:16 NKJV).

I don't understand many things about the incarnation, things that may be impossible for human beings to ever fully understand. But here's something I know: Through the incarnation, Jesus entered into human suffering—both in the ultimate sense that He took our sin and God's judgment on Himself and in the day-to-day sense that He made His dwelling in a human body with all its vulnerability to pain and brokenness. He wept. He sweated and prayed. He was beaten. He touched suffering people and power went out from Him to heal them. He did all of this to satisfy God's justice—and to live out God's love.

Here's another mystery about the incarnation: God was fully incarnated in Jesus, but He also dwells in each person who has received Him by faith. When these human beings who carry with them the Spirit of God enter a community where people are in pain—when they, like Christ, extend themselves into the suffering of others—they are in a place to share God's redemptive love. Vicarious suffering is redemptive. I'm not claiming that we have the power to redeem others the way Jesus did. But we become part of His work of drawing people to Him. What makes relocation so powerful is that it gives suffering people an opportunity to see and feel the deep love of God through another human being. God's love is incarnated in us—and through us it is transmitted into the lives of others.

But take caution. Some people start talking about God in them, and then they take it further and start talking about God speaking to them or working through them exclusively, and then suddenly they are acting like little gods. Christ *is* in us, and He does speak through us, but we go too far when we make ourselves the prophetic word itself instead of vessels of that word. We can actually end up thinking it's ours exclusively. It becomes an idol. Some people say, "I received the prophetic word from God and you didn't" or "God told me to tell you." God said, "Be still, and know that I am God" (Ps. 46:10), and revealed himself to Elijah in the still, small whisper (see 1 Kings 19:12). We can hear God's voice in the supportive words of a neighbor or the comforting words of a doctor. It is not about the person with the loudest shout. More often than not, someone is listening to their own loud voice, not God's.

When I first came back to Mendenhall, people would come by my office when they discovered I was a Bible teacher. These people were Christians who wanted to be discipled. One in particular, Miss Johnson, had started coming to my Bible class and desired to share the gospel with others in the community. She told me about an experience where she talked to a boy who listened intently to her words. The boy asked her what he had to do to be saved, and she told him to go back and hear the preacher. But that wasn't necessary at all. "Honey, *you* are the preacher!" I told her. The answer to the question of how to be saved is to believe in the Lord Jesus Christ. By sharing this message with others, we all become preachers of sorts.

When we realize that we bear God's image and that He lives in us, we want to draw closer to Him—and to His love. As His love grows in us, it overflows to others. We feel more of His love for others with the knowledge that He bore our sins and the sins of the world. His identification with us and our identification with Him make His love through us go out to the pain of others. As we bear that pain, it becomes redemptive to the person who is suffering. Our joy is filled in the fact that we can identify and empathize with that pain. Our ability to endure that pain stretches. We take His cross upon us. His burden is easy and the yoke is light. And through this we've expanded our ability to carry pain. That's why the disciples could say that they counted it a joy to suffer shame for His name. That's what being incarnational is about.

When we moved back to California in 1982, we bought a house in northwest Pasadena where there was death, violence, and drugs. Crack cocaine had just hit the streets, especially in our neighborhood. We knew it was a rough area, but we didn't know just how bad it was. Vera Mae began inviting the kids in the neighborhood to a Good News Club. We also invited some wealthy adults who lived outside the area to come to prayer meetings. During one prayer meeting, a young man from the neighborhood was shot right in front of our house. After the commotion was over, we went back inside and continued to pray. But the shooting not only left the young neighborhood boy dead, it also left emotional marks on my rich friends. Over the next days and weeks, they told their friends, co-workers, and relatives about what they had witnessed. As a result, our prayer meetings grew in attendance, attracting people concerned about what had happened and how they might help prevent such violence in the future. Everyone from professional baseball players to book publishers to college students gave their time and resources to make a positive difference.

Two of those people, Roland Hinds, and his wife, Lila, were among my and Vera Mae's best friends and supported us in our ministry. Others included Steve Lazarian, his son Stan, and his family. Always willing to assist, they founded The Door of Hope, a family shelter. Donna Roberts was another dear friend who I still visit every time I'm in California. I recently preached at the funeral for Pat Myers, another friend I made through those meetings. I was beyond blessed to experience such amazing relationships birthed out of these times of prayer.

Living in that community and inviting others to visit our home became the spark for development. Others have done the same. I can look across America and give you many examples of people who have moved into a community and taken on the pain of the people who live there.

—⁓—

So how do we live in a way that others can see Christ in us but not fall into the trap of making ourselves godlike? The answer is in the quality of the teaching we receive—and in our own diligence in seeking out the truth. Paul told Timothy to "be diligent to present yourself approved to God, a worker who does not need to be ashamed, rightly dividing the word of truth" (2 Tim. 2:15 NKJV). Unfortunately, not all teachers rightly divide the word of truth.

There will be those who sneak around among us, twisting God's Word and drawing out disciples to themselves. That's why it's important to carefully examine the things people tell us about God—and test those things against Scripture. Luke praised such testing: "Now the Berean Jews were of more noble character than those in Thessalonica, for they received the message with great eagerness and examined the Scriptures every day to see if what Paul said was true" (Acts 17:11). If the apostle Paul was not exempt from having his teaching held up against Scripture, our teachers today sure shouldn't be.

We can also go too far to the other side though. One Sunday a young woman at church sang a song that just sort of lifted me. It spoke to me and touched me somehow. So afterward I spoke to her and told her how much her singing meant to me. She said, "It wasn't me, it was all God." I don't think that's quite true. Sure, it all begins with God. This woman is created in His image, and He gave her the gift of a beautiful voice. But she had to work to develop that gift; she had to decide to use it in a way that honors God. That was her contribution. So it was God working through her, but that doesn't mean she wasn't involved. God used her voice to speak to my heart that morning. That's part of the mystery of incarnation.

The mystery here is that the God of all creation has called us to be part of His redemptive work. This should be our greatest joy. To be used by God should be our deepest longing and desire. Knowing we can do something for God is an awesome thought. This is the grace of God—that we can be a part of God's family, a part of the body of Christ. All we do must flow out of our gratitude for this unspeakable gift, for it is remarkable to think that He can flow His love through us (see 1 Cor. 9). One can have the gift of teaching or preaching or mercy or hospitality, but the greatest blessing is being able to share that gift with others. When Christ came down full of grace and truth, He imparted those gifts onto us. To live incarnationally means that we also continue to give these gifts away in order to edify the body of Christ.

I believe that the human dimension of God's work is very important. It's not that He couldn't accomplish anything He wanted to do without us, but He chooses to use what Paul called earthen vessels: "But we have this treasure in earthen vessels, that the excellence of the power may be of God and not of us" (2 Cor. 4:7 NKJV). This is what the young singer was probably trying to express, and I appreciate that. The power is of God. We are not the main force at work, yet we are involved. We are present. God uses us in one another's lives.

At a recent conference some of the young people I had met tried to convince me that they didn't really need a preacher. They're frustrated with traditional church leadership but believe in the priesthood of believers, which is all well and good. But they prefer a virtual church over a traditional one.

I told them, "That's going to be weak, because it's going to miss the incarnation. It will not have a human touch."

The writer of Hebrews gave us this exhortation: "And let us consider how we may spur one another on toward love and good deeds, not giving up meeting together, as some are in the habit of doing, but encouraging one another—and all the more as you see the Day approaching" (Heb. 10:24–25). That active presence of other believers contributes to God's work within us. Again, it's not that God needs us to complete what He is doing—but He allows that human dimension to be a part of His redemptive work. We are so quick, as human beings, to get our salvation and then make it personal. *It's all about Jesus and me.* What would happen if we organized with the expectation that God is going to use us in one another's lives—if we recognized the importance of those around us to our own spiritual growth?

—⚏—

Now let's get back to relocation, which is a specific kind of incarnation. Relocation is a way for us to enter into the pain of the people God has called us to serve. This idea of calling is important. I think God calls us in general ways and specific ways. In general, we're all called to make disciples. Then it can get a little more specific. Paul was called to carry the good news to the gentiles. That was still a pretty sweeping call. Anyone who wasn't a Jew was a gentile, so that was a lot of people. Paul couldn't go to all of them, so he had to narrow his focus. He knew his overall calling, so everything he did tied into that.

Then sometimes God would be even more specific:

When they came to the border of Mysia, they tried to enter Bithynia, but the Spirit of Jesus would not allow them to. So they passed by Mysia and went down to Troas. During the night Paul had a vision of a man of Macedonia standing and begging him, "Come over to Macedonia and help us." After Paul had seen the vision, we got ready at once to leave for Macedonia, concluding that God had called us to preach the gospel to them. (Acts 16:7–10)

The key, of course, is honing our skills in terms of listening to God's voice—that's how we can discern His call on our lives at different levels. Throughout Scripture, we read about God's concern for people who are vulnerable or suffering: the poor, the widows and orphans, the foreigners in the land, and so on. All Christians should feel a sense of calling to where there is pain in our society. Then if we hear something more specific from God, perhaps that requires some urgency, we should be willing to go to a different place. Maybe the call is like Paul's and it's about a certain group of people—the homeless, prisoners, people with AIDS, or whomever. Then our geographic location might not matter so much. The important thing would be to go where we can be incarnational with the particular type of people God has called us to reach.

Something I'm coming to believe is that God will carry out those things He is concerned about. If I have a will to obey Him by doing something in an area He is concerned about, He will get me to the place He wants me to be. It may take some time, and the journey may take me through several places along the way. Moses took forty years to get the Israelites to the place where God had called them to go. Moses was concerned at the beginning of that journey about how he would know that God was with them. He didn't want to go without God's presence. "And God said, 'I will be with you. And this will be the sign to you that it is I who have sent you: When you have brought the people out of Egypt, you will worship God on this mountain'" (Exod. 3:12). That's kind of a hard thing. The only way for Moses to know that God was with him was to finish the task God had called him to do—that would be the sign.

So when we say yes to God, sometimes we have to grow to believe He is with us like He promised—even if there is no sign of His presence until later. When we finish our task—when we arrive at that place He wants us to be—then we can see how much of a grace act it was for Him to bring us there. So in a sense, obedience opens up the grace. When we have the will to obey God, He affirms that and opens up His grace even more to us.

It fills me with joy to have many ministry friends who have grabbed ahold of this idea and live it out beautifully by living and serving in inner-city communities. I think if you ask any of them, they will say that relocation has been the most important element of their ministry and development. They will probably tell you that they've received more than they've given during all their years of loving hurting neighbors.

In recent years, groups like InnerCHANGE (founded by John Hayes), Word Made Flesh (directed by Leroy Barber), and the Simple Way (Shane Claiborne's community) have formed to minister incarnationally in suffering communities around the nation and world. One of many wonderful things I've noticed about these groups is that they also embody the redistribution idea—they call people to live at the level of others in the community, so that extra resources can be shared. They're challenging people to give up some things so they're able to better share their lives and their wealth with people who need it.

I've been thinking recently about God's judgment—and how it usually fell on the Israelites during their more prosperous times. And even today, when God's people have more wealth—and when they use that wealth to satisfy themselves by living lavishly—that's generally when His judgment comes. I've always had a great sense of urgency in terms of reaching out to the poor. More and more, though, I'm developing an urgent concern for the wealthy. Relocation and redistribution aren't just for the benefit of those who receive the human and economic resources of people coming into the community. They are for the benefit of those who choose not to hoard the resources they have—who decide instead to forgo some of those material things and come to live next to and eat with and know the people God has called them to love.

God does not necessarily call everyone to relocate into a poor community, though He wants us all to be a blessing to the poor, have a special love for them, and utilize our resources for them. He calls us to be good stewards of the resources He has entrusted to us and to help both the rich and the poor to realize it is more blessed to give than to receive.

John McGill, a great friend of mine and successful businessman in the California food industry, helped me so much in the early days of my ministry. He didn't give me large amounts of money, but he did give me his time, visiting me when I was in Mississippi. And he taught me something I will always remember. He said,

> John, we are workers and brothers and sisters together in this ministry, and God has me serving the needs of the people in Southern California in terms of food and has given me a good return on my stewardship and investment. The biggest deal here is that I work hard, and I encourage my workers to work hard. My money is a part of my stewardship. Really, I'm stewarding my energy and my time. We all have the same amount of time, and I use mine and I sweat—and that's my blood. So when I'm giving you money and sharing my wealth with you, I'm really sharing my blood and sharing my life.

My good friend Howard Ahmanson does the same. I'm always telling him what he ought to be thinking about and doing, and he always comes back to me saying, "John, you have the same amount of time as I have." Time, as well as wealth, must be stewarded in a way that is pleasing to God.

But the truth is that there is enough time and enough wealth to go around. The people in the churches every Sunday outnumber the people who are on the streets and the number of people on welfare. If the church took up the responsibility of caring for the poor, of living incarnationally, of participating in the unspeakable gift of giving, our world would look much different from the way it does today. Justice is a stewardship issue, caring for the poor is a stewardship issue, loving our neighbor as we love ourselves is a stewardship issue. We have the resources, but our priorities aren't there yet. If I could call the church to task on one more thing in the years I have left, it would be to start stewarding our resources in a way that adheres to the will of God and is in line with His kingdom. We can look to the apostle Paul's example: "I have been crucified with Christ and I no longer live, but Christ lives in me. The life I now live in the body, I live by faith in the Son of God, who loved me and gave himself for me" (Gal. 2:20). I long to see the church give up its power and privilege the way Jesus did when He came to earth to give us the greatest of gifts. Now *that* would be incarnational living.

7

Real Justice

Sometimes I look at the Bible and think all God is about is justice. Consider just this small sample of Scripture verses that declare God's commitment to justice: "For the LORD loves justice" (Ps. 37:28 NASB); "I know that the LORD secures justice for the poor and upholds the cause of the needy" (Ps. 140:12); "For the LORD is a God of justice" (Isa. 30:18 NKJV); "What does the LORD require of you but to do justice, to love kindness, and to walk humbly with your God?" (Mic. 6:8 NASB). Clearly, justice matters to God. But what does it look like? When we talk about justice, what do we really mean?

Justice is an economic and stewardship issue. When Psalm 24:1 says, "The earth is the LORD's, and everything in it," that's a justice statement. The way we utilize the resources we've been given determines whether we are being just.

In many ways, black theology and white theology in churches in America have been like two sides of a coin when it comes to thinking about justice and redemption. To put it in very general terms, white theology (especially white evangelical theology) has tended to focus on the personal side of redemption. Emphasis has been placed on evangelism, salvation, and individual spiritual growth and holiness—with the Bible being regarded as a devotional book that inspires believers individually. This focus is terribly important, of course, because it highlights the relationships between people and God. It also recognizes a crucial and painful truth about justice: apart from the blood of Christ, justice is bad news for sinful human beings. At least it's bad news if we're talking about the type of justice that demands that a penalty be paid when a wrong is done.

The Old Testament is filled with instructions about this kind of justice—certain sins result in certain punishments or means of atonement (see, for example, Lev. 4–6 and 19–20). The specifics of some of these crimes and punishments may seem strange to us today, but we're not unfamiliar with the general concept. If a ball goes through a neighbor's window, the child who threw it will likely be disciplined by their parents and may also be required to pay to have the broken window replaced. We expect people who commit more serious crimes to spend time in jail, and many times those individuals must also pay a monetary fine or make some kind of restitution to their victims.

Christians come down on both sides of the death penalty debate when it comes to our human criminal justice system, but make no mistake—in God's justice system, "The wages of sin is death" (Rom. 6:23). I don't know about you, but apart from the blood of Christ, I'm not particularly eager to see this kind of justice carried out in my life. The good news of the gospel is that God has made a way to satisfy the demands of justice through sacrifice and redemption rather than through judgment and condemnation.

—⁓—

Black theology has a very different take on both redemption and justice, in part because much of it has been developed in response to white oppression. In terms of redemption—or liberation—black theology builds on the "Let my people go!" model of Moses. It celebrates God's history of delivering His people from slavery and oppression and regards redemption as communal as well as individual.

104

As black Christians, we almost always see religion as something that uplifts people, and the Bible is considered a textbook for living. Black theology doesn't specify that blacks and whites should be separate, but sadly it has turned out that way.

We never should have needed or wanted black theology. If the church in America more generally had arrived at a theology that included an increased understanding of God's redemptive work, we all would be better off. White theology, however, has a serious problem: because the church added "racial" to reconciliation as part of the gospel in an effort to accommodate racism, the stream was poisoned. Even today, many church leaders maintain that it is inappropriate or even evil to organize their congregations to get them to protest injustice. Thus, the struggle to understand biblical truth about justice and redemption continues.

Black theology is alien to most white people—and if they hear a little bit of it in a negative context or out of context, they're likely to have a serious problem with it. Racism creates anger. Because of the blatant racism of the past and its common occurrence today, many white Christians do just enough social good in the black community to salve their consciences while maintaining imperialistic theology. They do just enough to get by without repentance.

This tension became quite apparent in regard to the riots that took place in Ferguson, Missouri, after a white police officer shot and killed an unarmed black man. The white community sees the reaction of the black community and thinks it is too strong, too violent, and too much. But we in the black community feel we have been oppressed too long and that the changes boasted are, in reality, a far cry from the rhetoric and the legislation. So, of course, we tend to react strongly. Both sides are yelling too loudly to listen to one another. We have accommodated the racism and the segregation in society for so long that we have lost our ability to hear or understand one another. We remain aloof, each failing to relate to the agony of the other's pain and both adamantly resisting what God requires:

repentance and forgiveness. Without these things, everyone forfeits the cleansing blood of Jesus to mend the past and current hurts. Our efforts to be in right relationship with God and in sincere fellowship with one another are crippled.

This illustrates a problem with black theology—or at least black Christian practice. Unfortunately, often the black community is very slow to forgive, expecting white people to prove their repentance by their works. We know from Jesus's teaching on prayer—"Forgive us our debts, as we forgive our debtors" (Matt. 6:12 NKJV)—how essential it is for us to forgive one another. We also know that "all have sinned and fall short of the glory of God" (Rom. 3:23 NKJV), and in America it's pretty safe to say that blacks and whites and the other ethnic groups represented have all sinned against one another. So all parties need to repent, and all parties need to forgive. This is the only way out of the hostility and division we have long accommodated in many different kinds of churches.

But I've gotten a little off track . . . besides having a different focus when it comes to redemption, black theology also has a different—or at least another—emphasis when it comes to justice. Old Testament justice laws aren't just about punishing sin; they're also about preventing oppression. They're about making sure that each person in the community is cared for and given an opportunity to flourish. Instructions about gleaning (see Lev. 23:22) and the year of Jubilee (see Lev. 25:8–55), for instance, demonstrate God's desire that the poor should have ways to feed themselves and chances to get out from under debilitating debt. We often refer to this type of justice as social justice, and this is something that has been important to the black church in America. This is the type of justice I've frequently spoken and written about—it's a social and economic concept that moves people in a community toward mutual concern and both individual and collective development.

For the most part, in the past the white church in America has not embraced this kind of justice thinking. There are exceptions, of course. The Quakers and Mennonites, for instance, have always put a strong emphasis on justice and equality within their communities. But their influence isn't very widespread, and for a long time there wasn't a national call to make justice a priority in the church. The Catholic Church also has had a little bit of an advantage in this because they've maintained the idea of the parish—the congregation being grounded in the community. As communities around individual Catholic churches changed demographically, some of those congregations developed greater concern for the justice issues that affected their newer parishioners.

Something I'm sensing now, though—something that gives me a great deal of hope and joy—is a growing commitment to social justice among evangelical Christians. For hundreds of years, slavery and the legacy of slavery kept justice from being a functioning part of many churches, but I can see things changing now. We haven't quite gotten to the place yet where we fully grasp how justice is the very foundation of God's intentions for the world, but good things are happening.

I've encountered several churches that do a wonderful job of pursuing social justice—not just reaching out to help the poor in their communities with food, clothing, and other physical needs, but also welcoming those individuals into their congregations as brothers and sisters. The congregation at Calvary Church in Minneapolis, Minnesota, has so identified with the poor and made people feel so welcome that many of the homeless in the community worship at this church. One of the things the church does is open its doors on Sunday afternoon and invite the community to eat and watch football there. Many of the shelters aren't open on Sunday, so this gives the homeless folks a place to spend the day. It also provides an opportunity for fellowship that doesn't revolve around the wealthier members giving something to the poorer members.

Tenth Presbyterian Church in Philadelphia, Pennsylvania, is another great example. This is one of those city churches where many of the members lived out in the suburbs and commuted in for services and activities. Well, after hearing me preach and inviting me to visit their church for a missions conference, the pastor, the late Dr. James Montgomery Boice, and his wife, Linda, were inspired to move into the urban neighborhood where the church is located. He and Linda started an elite school there—not for the children of the rich families who attended the church but for the poor children who lived in the community around the church building. She taught at this school, City Center Academy, to help provide these children with the best possible education. The Boices did a wonderful job and stayed at the church until James passed away. The school has now merged with other schools in the area. This congregation has become somewhat integrated, and many of the black middle-class members, as well as some of the wealthy whites who attend, are concerned about the homeless in the area. They started doing various kinds of outreach on Saturdays, and eventually added a third Sunday service geared toward the homeless people they were interacting with. It's a real worship service, attended by some of the more affluent members as well. I have talked to some of the homeless people who attend it, and this is their church.

These are just a couple examples of what is happening throughout America's urban communities. This authentic outreach to the poor and neglected is working. Signs of true justice taking place through a holistic approach to the gospel—the whole church engaging the whole community—are evident throughout the United States. While I am a big champion of parachurch organizations, I really want to see local congregations adopt this cause all over this nation. I want worship and social justice to be done in the same building. People coming together across ethnicities and cultural barriers, as well as socioeconomic and class status, to integrate the poor into mainstream society is the image of justice I want to see.

So I'm encouraged, and I want to celebrate the light that is breaking on the scene. I want to see us continue on this journey toward developing and practicing theology that embraces both the redemptive justice of the cross and social and economic justice in our communities. If I can say, at the end of my life, that I lived to see justice welcomed back into the church in America, that will be a wonderful thing. As a young person, that wasn't a statement I thought I'd ever be able to make.

―――

As excited as I am about what I see happening around me, I'm still not done thinking about justice and seeking to deepen my understanding of what it is. The two sides of justice that I've been discussing here both stem from one perspective: What does justice look like for human beings? There's nothing wrong with that, but it recently occurred to me to turn that question around and ask, What does justice look like from God's perspective? As I mentioned before, as human beings, we don't really want justice in its strictest sense—because we would be condemned. But God, who is holy and perfect, has no reason to fear justice. He desires it. According to the Bible, He loves it. Remember those verses I mentioned at the start of the chapter (Ps. 37:28; 140:12; Isa. 30:18; Mic. 6:8)?

One of the greatest biblical stories of justice is in the book of Ruth. Nestled right between Judges, a book filled with God's justice, and 1 Samuel, which lays out the establishment of the kingdom of Israel, we find perhaps the best example of love, justice, and grace all wrapped together. And if you haven't read through the whole story recently, put down this book for a while and spend some time in the book of Ruth.

Israel in Old Testament times had systems—such as the principle of gleaning—built to make real justice happen. Leviticus 19:9–10 says, "When you reap the harvest of your land, you shall not wholly reap the corners of your field, nor shall you gather the gleanings of your harvest. And you shall not glean your vineyard, nor shall you gather every grape of your vineyard; you shall leave them for the poor and the stranger: I am the Lord your God" (NKJV). In the book of Ruth, Boaz, a rich landowner, didn't just harvest all of his grain and then give it away, he left some for the poor, like Ruth, to glean. It was an act of grace that allowed Ruth and her mother-in-law, Naomi, to have dignity, to work, not just receive handouts.

But the story is more than that. Boaz also became her kinsman-redeemer. He took on Ruth's burden and restored her, giving her the greatest gift—the whole farm—by taking her as his wife. In many ways, this parallels another essential part of justice—Jesus Christ taking on the sins of humanity, giving us the greatest gift of eternal life, and setting us free from our miserable state of sin. As Boaz gave to his bride, Ruth, an immeasurable and undeserved gift, so Christ gives to His bride, the church, the immeasurable and undeserved gift of salvation.

And out of this relationship between Boaz and Ruth, Jesse, the father of David, was born. Boaz's seemingly small act of justice birthed the greatest earthly king of Israel and eventually the Savior and restorer of the whole world. Out of the deep love between Naomi and Ruth and the grace and justice of Boaz, a kingdom was built. The greatest love story in the Bible is also the greatest story of justice.

I'm sure that my understanding of justice is not yet complete, but the best I've been able to discern so far through prayer, study, and much thought is this: justice is any act of reconciliation that restores any part of God's creation back to its original intent, purpose, or image. When I think about justice that way, it doesn't surprise me at all that God loves it. It includes both the acts of social justice and the restorative justice found on the cross. I love it too, and I can't wait to see what it looks like when God's redemptive work in the world is complete—when His kingdom has come, and we finally have a chance to live in the relationships with Him and one another that He intended for us from the beginning.

This view of justice also helps me to better understand this teaching of Jesus: "Whatever you did for one of the least of these brothers and sisters of mine, you did for me" (Matt. 25:40). God has always wanted the vulnerable in society to be cared for. He never intended for them to languish in poverty, abuse, slavery, homelessness, or other types of devastation. When we care for individuals who are trapped in these ways—when we show them love and help them move toward freedom and wholeness—we participate in bringing a little part of God's kingdom back into alignment with His greater plan. We do justice and God smiles.

8

Spencer

Even as a young child, my son Spencer was extraordinarily kind, and it was that kindness that prompted me to search for God. I remember having a vague sense that there was a God—that He was out there someplace—but I only went to church every once in a while, when Vera Mae insisted. But three- or four-year-old Spencer, who came home from his Bible classes joyful and eager to share what he was learning, made me want to find out more about this God he was getting to know. Spencer's ability to love intrigued me more than anything. He wanted us to pray before our meals, and he sang Christian songs like "Jesus Loves the Little Children," proclaiming God loved all the children—red and yellow, black and white. He also invited me to attend class with him.

My own son's love for me led me to where I could discover and experience God's love for me. I learned later that there was another motivation for Spencer's invitation: his teacher had offered a prize to any child who brought someone to Sunday school. Spencer knew he was going to get that prize, because he knew I would come if he asked me. At that time, he was more excited about the prize than my salvation! Whatever the reason, Spencer was the human instrument God used to lead me to Him.

In Mendenhall as a teenager, Spencer took on a different kind of leadership—being a pioneer in desegregation efforts. He and four of my other children were in the first wave of black students to voluntarily integrate the white school. That experience was so miserable for them, Vera Mae and I didn't make them stay after those first couple of years. But when mandatory integration came to the state, Spencer enrolled in Mendenhall High. Spencer was a gifted, accomplished athlete who excelled at every sport he tried: football, baseball, basketball, and track. He was versatile and always stayed very fit. He was especially skilled at basketball. During Spencer's third year at Mendenhall High, the school's basketball team won the state championship, and he got the game ball for being the most valuable player on the team. The one white boy on the team was the son of our insurance agent. So there was some goodwill there, and that helped our work in the community.

Later, Spencer graduated from Belhaven College in Jackson—likely the first black to graduate from there. Belhaven came to love having Spencer as a student. When he first started, people didn't persecute him, but they didn't love him either, mainly because they didn't know him yet. But they grew to love him, and the school even named an award after him, placing a plaque on the chapel pulpit to honor him. I will always appreciate Belhaven for how they embraced my son.

Although Spencer became a leader in reconciliation, there was a time when he struggled hard with love and forgiveness. It was after I was beaten in the Rankin County Jail in Brandon on February 7, 1970. Vera Mae brought him and the rest of my children to see me in the hospital. I still looked horrible—all swollen and bruised, bandaged up, and filled with tubes. Joanie ran right out of the room in a rage, yelling that she would hate white people for the rest of her life. Spencer's reaction was much quieter, but he was also angry. Soon it wasn't just the white highway patrol officers he was mad at. It was me too. He told me I'd become a different person after the beating.

He thought I'd lost my fire because I was talking about forgiveness. It seemed like I was a more submissive person now, and he didn't like that. He had to get to know his daddy all over again—and even though he still loved me, he didn't like the new version of me as much as he had liked the old version. Later, he would look back on that time, and he said he could see how something supernatural was happening in me. He eventually embraced the idea of loving and forgiving our enemies, but right after the beating, he wasn't ready to forgive. He was too angry about what those men had done to his father. It wasn't just the beating. He had also experienced rejection by whites during school integration in Mendenhall—but what happened in Brandon really added to his anger.

Because Spencer was our firstborn, and that has strong significance in African American homes, Vera Mae raised him to take over for me. Dinner was always a special time at our house, and Vera Mae ordered the table just the way she wanted it. Our youngest girl, Elizabeth, would sit between her mother and me. I would sit at one end of the table, and Vera Mae would place herself where she could easily come and go from the kitchen. The other children, except for Spencer, sat around the table in order of age. Spencer sat at the end opposite me. If I was away, he would sit in my place. The other kids recognized how we groomed Spencer to lead, so when Vera Mae and I would talk with them about a decision we had made, they would often ask, "Does Spencer know about this?" A decision wasn't final until Spencer was in the loop.

Some children, when they want something, will go to one parent or the other trying to get an easy yes. Not Spencer. He usually came to Vera Mae and me together. He would tell us he wanted to talk with us, and we knew it was significant. Spencer even grew up to look like me. When he got older, into his forties, his hair started to thin, and he shaved his head. If it was good enough for Michael Jordan, it was good enough for him, he said. We took a picture together when he was balding, and we looked like twins.

Our hopes for Spencer extended beyond our family. We wished for him to go into the ministry as well but tried not to push too hard. I wanted to let him find his own way. I think he felt the pressure anyway. He didn't like having that weight on him, and for a while he really worked to avoid being part of the ministry.

Immediately after college Spencer decided to start his own business. He liked photography, so he thought maybe he could make a living taking portraits of people. That didn't work out, so he filled in for one of the secretaries at the ministry doing some typing for a while. Working all those hours on the typewriter stirred in him a desire to write. One of his teachers once told us he was the best student she had ever had in English. He didn't talk a lot during his school days, but he liked words. He did a lot of reading back then too and especially loved historical books.

Spencer still wasn't ready to jump headlong into the ministry, so he and his brother Phillip started a business where they rebuilt and refurbished car batteries. They would drive down to New Orleans to pick up old batteries for about a dollar, and then they would fix

116

them up and sell them for a decent profit. That worked pretty well until intense competition emerged. The call to writing was getting stronger for Spencer, so he came back to work for Voice of Calvary editing our newsletter, which was called *A Quiet Revolution.*

By this time Voice of Calvary's board was starting to see our work as having a national, and even international, scope. It was still grounded in grassroots neighborhood development but was growing into a bigger role and helping to bring this kind of ministry to communities all over the world. So it didn't really matter where I lived—and Spencer didn't have to be in a particular place either. So I had the aspiration for him to continue developing his writing and start doing some speaking—but I didn't have a sense of place attached to that.

When Vera Mae and I moved out to Pasadena, California, in 1982, Spencer continued to work at Voice of Calvary, while my daughters Priscilla and Elizabeth attended boarding school. We did some of the same kinds of community organizing and evangelism work in Pasadena that we had done in Mississippi, but we also started the John and Vera Mae Perkins Foundation for Reconciliation, Justice, and Christian Community Development. In 1992, the foundation launched *Urban Family*, a magazine geared toward bringing the vision of Christian community development to the black Christian community. Spencer and a white Voice of Calvary staff member named Chris Rice became *Urban Family*'s editors, and eventually we spun off the magazine as its own ministry. Spencer and Chris, who wrote the book *More Than Equals* together, eventually changed the name of the magazine to *Reconcilers Fellowship* and started to do reconciliation workshops on top of putting out the magazine. They had their share of struggles—which I learned about much later—but they were doing important work.

Spencer would have said, though, that his more important ministry was in and through the Antioch community. Antioch had started back in the mid-1980s when a group of folks from Voice of Calvary, including Spencer, Chris, and Joanie, started meeting together for

Bible study. They wanted to see what would happen if they took the Bible—and especially the Sermon on the Mount—seriously enough to follow its instructions.

Earlier in his life, Spencer had strayed away from a deep walk with God. He stayed within the framework of what you might call being a "good" Christian, but his faith just wasn't as strong or as intimate as it had been. By the time this Bible study began, he had married a wonderful Mennonite woman, Nancy Horst, and his faith had been rekindled. He was one of the leaders of the study. After meeting together for a couple of years and wrestling with the Scriptures together, this group decided to pool their resources, buy a big yellow house in the community, and all move in together. They wanted to experience a deeper Christianity than what they generally saw in the society around them. This community was extremely important to Spencer because he loved people so much. For years he had been getting to know and love volunteers and interns as they spent time in Jackson, but then they would leave. He wanted love to last forever. So they developed this intentional community where they were going to stay together for the long haul.

Now, I was never part of that community officially, but I would visit them and could tell they had a really good quality of life together. There were sometimes as many as twenty-nine people living in the community, including several of my grandchildren. I loved how when I'd visit, we'd sit around the dinner table, and we'd start out talking about some event or another—just something that had happened in the community or in the world—and pretty soon we'd be talking about theology. Spencer loved to discuss ideas. So we'd talk about discipleship and reconciliation and all sorts of other topics. They really understood what it meant to be a community, and they had a rich life experience together.

They never could hold on to money though. All of my kids, and especially Spencer, seem to have a sense that if they're doing the right thing, the money will follow. They get that from Vera Mae, and I agree with it—to a certain extent. The thing is, I also believe it's important to have good decision-making processes in place to manage the resources God gives you. What happened with Antioch and the magazine was that God would provide—sometimes through Vera Mae and me at the foundation and sometimes through other sources—and the people at the Antioch community would give the money to help others. Their motivation was good. They felt the pain of people's needs, and they always wanted to meet those needs. Unfortunately, their compassion sometimes made them naive. They would lend money to people who never had any intention of paying them back. Or they would hire someone who wasn't qualified to do the job, just because they wanted that person to have a paycheck. So money was always a struggle—and I know that burden rested heavily on Spencer.

While we were in Pasadena, I decided that when I turned sixty-five, I wanted to give up my administrative responsibilities and turn my full attention to preaching and teaching. I wanted to move back to Jackson and undergird what Spencer and the rest of the people in the Antioch community were doing. They had a little bit of youth ministry going on and were doing some workshops and internships, but a lot of their energy was directed toward working out their life together as a community. Vera Mae and I wanted to come alongside them and help grow their outward ministry. So we turned the work in Pasadena over to our son Derek, our daughter Priscilla, and Rudy Carrasco. We spent a year in Dallas so I could travel to promote CCDA, and then we moved into the house next door to Antioch. It was wonderful to get up each morning and know we could go over and visit our children and grandchildren. Spencer and Nancy had their three kids—Johnathan, Jubilee, and April Joy. Joanie had married Ron Potter, and they adopted Varah and then Karah. That was a happy time for me.

Spencer was struggling, though, which was hard for me to watch. He and I went out to Colorado Springs at one point to do a father-son radio program with Dr. James Dobson at Focus on the Family. Dr. Dobson and I had been friends for quite a while, and he asked us to come and talk about the black community and the need to see more authentic Christianity among African Americans. So we taped the programs and then took a tour of the Focus on the Family facilities. Spencer saw their success—the efficiency of their systems and how they had plenty of resources to do what they needed to do—and I think that really discouraged him. He felt like, back at Antioch and through Reconcilers Fellowship, they were doing work that was just as important, but they didn't have the resources they needed.

A couple of weeks later, Spencer injured himself playing basketball and wound up with his leg in a cast. Someone told me later that shortly after his injury, he was trying to do something that required physical strength, but he couldn't. He just broke down and wept. He must have felt defeated—like he had done everything that was required of him as a Christian, but he and his community still couldn't quite make things work. I think he felt like they had failed, and that ate at him. Around that same time, he came to visit Vera Mae and me one morning. We sat together for a good hour or more, but he didn't really say much. When he left, Vera Mae and I wondered what he had wanted. I imagine he was thinking about asking us to give the ministry greater financial support, but he never brought that up.

Right after that, in January 1998, Reconcilers Fellowship held a conference with more than three hundred attendees. Professors, InterVarsity staff members, and other campus ministers from colleges and universities around the United States gathered in Jackson to talk about reconciliation. I missed the first part of it because I was in California for a few days, but I flew back in time to speak at a workshop Saturday morning. On Saturday morning, during a plenary session, Spencer collapsed. The whole conference stopped and everybody prayed over him, and then he was whisked off to the hospital. We found out later it was a blood-sugar-related episode. He was exhausted and physically weak after that, but he came back to the conference so he and Chris Rice could give their keynote address.

People still talk about what he said on that Saturday night. He spoke about grace. He emphasized the need for all minority Christians—especially African American Christians—to forgive white folks, and not just the white folks who prove they "deserve" to be forgiven. He talked about how we minority Christians often play the "race card," but instead we need to play the "grace card." It was the first time I had ever heard that saying—grace card—and even though a movie has since come out by that name, I give Spencer credit for coining it.

The sermon he gave that night is included in the revised and expanded edition of *More Than Equals*. He talked about the church needing to create a culture of grace and how people can hear God's truth better when it isn't all mixed up in human judgment. He and Chris shared their own struggles and how they'd had to learn to forgive each other and release each other before they could continue to minister together. It was a hopeful night. It felt like a new beginning for Spencer, Reconcilers Fellowship, and Antioch.

Tragically, Spencer suffered a massive heart attack just three days later at the age of forty-four. He was at home in his study at the time. We lived just a few doors down from him (Antioch had expanded into several houses on the same block), so when I saw the emergency vehicles in front of the house, I ran over and helped get him into the ambulance. I wanted to get in with him, but the paramedics wouldn't let me. So I drove behind the ambulance to the hospital. When we got there, the ER staff took him into a room and worked on him for about twenty minutes. Then the doctor came out and told me he was gone. He said that Spencer was already gone when he arrived at the hospital, but they thought because he was so young, maybe they could save him. Even after the doctor told me that, he went back into the room and worked on Spencer a little more. Nobody wanted to let him go, I guess.

A little while later the doctor led me into the room where Spencer lay. I remembered somebody once saying something about touching a deceased person while they were still warm—before all the life had gone from them. So I walked around to Spencer's head and touched his face. It felt like he was a baby again. That was one of the most traumatic experiences I've had in my life. The grief I felt in that moment is indescribable. This was my baby—the first person who ever really belonged to me—and he was dead. He was gone.

Then I had to get back in the car, drive home, and tell Vera Mae that our firstborn son was dead. I've never done anything as difficult as that. Vera Mae didn't want to believe me; it sort of seemed like she *couldn't* believe me at first. She was supposed to teach a Bible class at four o'clock that evening, and she kept saying, "I'm gonna do my Bible class. I'm gonna do my Bible class." She said she couldn't go to the hospital because she had to teach her class. I guess that Bible class was a way to express her dedication to God—or maybe just a way to avoid the reality of what I was saying. Our world was destroyed that day—our hearts were broken, our vision for the future was shattered, and we didn't know what we were going to do.

My reaction to not knowing what to do was to try to do everything. After I finally convinced Vera Mae to come to the hospital with me, I let our other kids and some friends take her back to the house while I went on to the funeral home. I had made a pre-arrangement for my Uncle Bud's burial, even though he was still living. I had that transferred to Spencer. I thought I was helping—just doing what had to be done. I found out later that by not consulting Spencer's wife, Nancy, about these arrangements, I had hurt her deeply—and rightfully so. I didn't mean to, but I could see, looking back, how my thoughtlessness hurt her.

It was amazing how many of our friends came to Spencer's wake and funeral. Rich friends, poor friends, friends from down the street and across the country—they were all there with us. At the wake, there was a time for people to share their thoughts. I got up and said to God, out loud in front of everybody, "God, I'm really mad at You. You took my son. I would have liked to have given him back to You, but You took him, and I didn't have a chance." I don't know if I could have voluntarily given up Spencer, but my words came out of my emotion and my feelings of loss and anger. As I spoke them, I thought of two things.

I thought about what missionary Jim Elliot had said about giving up what you can't keep in order to gain what you can't lose, and I decided to ask God for something. At the wake, I said, "God, You took my son. Would You give him back to me tonight? Would You give him back so I can give him to You?"

I also thought about this verse of Scripture: "Truly, truly, I say to you, unless a grain of wheat falls into the earth and dies, it remains alone; but if it dies, it bears much fruit" (John 12:24 NASB).

At the wake and the funeral, I also said, "God, I would like to give my son back to You tonight as a seed of reconciliation, so that from this seed, many others will grow. I pray that reconciliation will sprout all over this nation, and my son's death will not have been in vain." It helped me to do that—to think of Spencer's death as something that could bring about much good in the world. I didn't know how exactly that would happen, but I asked God for it and waited to see what He would do.

Losing Spencer was the worst blow Vera Mae and I had ever suffered—the most terrible pain we'd ever felt. But we grieved differently. Before Spencer died, Vera Mae was always energetic—always doing something. She was as much a workaholic as I was. If she wasn't driving a truck or running the tractor, she was out playing educational games with the kids, teaching them to fish, and being actively involved in all they did. She always kept going. After Spencer died, she hardly got out of bed. When she did get up, sometimes I would find her in the kitchen, just standing at the window and crying. You see, after we moved back to Jackson, Spencer would come see us at our house often. When he'd get to our gate, he'd call out "Momma! Momma!" to let Vera Mae know he was coming.

One time when I found her standing by the sink weeping, she said, "I'll never hear that voice again." She was just longing to hear him call out to her one more time. Losing Spencer almost destroyed her.

It also created a great disruption in our relationship—and in my relationship with Nancy. Both Vera Mae and Nancy were overwhelmed and pretty much paralyzed by their grief. Because I wasn't weeping and mourning the same way they were, they felt like I wasn't taking Spencer's death as seriously as they were. But that wasn't it. I was hurting too, but I had a mission—I was thinking about how I could honor my son's memory. If I'm honest, I have to admit that even though I had made a commitment to reconciliation after what happened in the Brandon jail, once Spencer and Chris committed to a ministry of reconciliation—and Glenn Kehrein and Raleigh Washington were writing about it too—I kind of let it go onto the back burner. Of course, I was always working on reconciliation through CCDA, but my own personal drive to be a reconciler had lessened somewhat. So once again, Spencer had a big impact on who I would become. After his wake, for a while I wondered, *Who is going to do this? Who is going to carry on his ministry of reconciliation?* Then I realized that I needed to do it. I needed to make reconciliation a priority in my life again—and at the same time I would be honoring Spencer's memory.

I started turning over in my mind what I should do. I thought about creating a training center to carry on the teaching ministry, but I didn't want to spend the rest of my life raising money. So I went back and forth in my mind for a few months, trying to make a decision. Then in mid-1998, a few months after Spencer died, Antioch decided they were going to break up and put up their property for sale. Nancy and the kids were planning to move to Pennsylvania, where her family was, and Joanie and Ron were talking about moving across town. It was like all my dreams for my future just kept crashing down. I continued thinking and praying—and now I was wondering, *Should I buy this property and build the center here?* I wanted to, but I thought it was going to cost too much money to buy and renovate it.

Then one night I had a dream. I dreamed that people from all over the nation—from the east and the west—had come to Jackson and said, "We want to help you build the center. We want to make it happen." I dreamed that they were there in the parking lot, with their trucks full of supplies, ready to help, but they couldn't get in. There was nobody there to open the gate to the fenced-in property.

That dream was so vivid that I jumped up out of bed and went to the window. This was about three o'clock in the morning, and of course nobody was there. But that vision was still so strong and powerful. In my mind I could see those people out there waiting to get in. I'd jumped up so fast that I woke up Vera Mae. When I went back to bed, I said to her, "Honey, let's buy this property and build a youth center and dedicate it to Spencer's life."

She said, "Okay, let's do it."

That wasn't like her at all. The next thing she said sounded a little more like the Vera Mae I knew: "Where are you going to get the money?"

I reminded her about an insurance policy and some CDs we had. They were supposed to be for our retirement and to take care of her if something ever happened to me, but she didn't even blink when I suggested we cash them in and use the money to buy the property—so that's what we did.

Pretty soon, our first volunteer group—from Ginghamsburg United Methodist Church in Ohio—arrived. When the volunteers pulled into the parking lot of the property we had purchased, I realized that dream I'd had was unfolding. The Ginghamsburg group brought truckloads of doors and other supplies in their first trip and came back sixteen more times after that. Their work included fixing up an old duplex, which we have since used as our volunteer house, the same place where all those groups that I dreamed about still come and stay today.

Our family, in agreement with others in our ministry, decided to call the new center built by the volunteers the Spencer Perkins Center of Reconciliation and Development. My friend Lowell Noble started doing workshops there. In a way the center saved me from grief. At the same time, it's how I do my grieving. When I'm out in the yard pulling up grass or inside working on a building or teaching a group of young people about reconciliation and justice, I'm thinking about Spencer. I'm thinking about him, feeling the pain of him not being here, and hoping that his death has made me more committed to Christ and to the ministry of reconciliation.

Sometimes, when people who haven't lost a child try to comfort me, they say something like, "John, you're going to get over it. You'll be okay."

I know they mean well, but I tell them, "I really don't want to get over it." They're asking me to do something I don't think I can do—and that I don't want to do. I want to keep the memories of my child in my life. Of course, I don't want to be paralyzed by this loss. I want to be able to function. If that's what they mean by getting over it, then yes, I want that. As time goes by, I want to get to a point where I can talk about Spencer's death without breaking up. But I never want to forget my child. I don't even want all of the pain to go away.

That's why I rush to people now when I hear they've lost a child. I remember how it felt to have people trying to talk to me when they didn't have any idea of the pain. So I want to be there to say to a grieving parent, "I know that pain. I live every day with that pain. You don't get over it. But you can learn to endure it—you can even learn to do something positive with it." I can credit these comforting words of wisdom to a dear friend of mine, Pastor John Huffman.

Spencer is buried in a beautiful old cemetery about a mile from my house. It covers about twenty acres of land and is one of the older cemeteries in Jackson. His grave lies in the shade of a tree and is marked with a plaque that says, "Well done, thou good and faithful servant." I go often to visit his grave and take care of the flowers and just meditate. I know Spencer is in heaven—I don't think he's there in the cemetery. But I like to go there and spend time with my memories of him. I have such a deep sense of gratitude for him being the human instrument that brought me to Christ. Sometimes I wonder if that was part of his mission. I have trouble knowing how to express this part, because I don't want to make it seem like it's about my importance, but sometimes I think that Spencer's mission might have been a little bit like John the Baptist's. Maybe my mission and Spencer's mission were tied together, and he was the one who went ahead of me, even though I was his father. He was ahead of me in coming to know the Lord, and then he led the way for me in this reconciliation ministry that has been the focus of these last years of my life.

When I think about the role Spencer has played in everything I've done that matters, I understand that the length of one's life is not important; the connection a person makes to the will of God and the mission of the kingdom is important. "Come Thou Fount of Every Blessing" became Spencer's favorite hymn in the last years of his life, and it has become mine as well. Sometimes I sit at Spencer's grave and think about how I want to be faithful in the mission I've taken over from him. Vera Mae and I own the two plots next to Spencer's. Someday we'll be buried there beside him. When that day comes, I hope that he, along with my mother, will be able to tell me that I did well with the time I was given—time that went on much longer than theirs did. I hope they'll be proud of me. As I think of him and my mother waiting for me in heaven, I especially love the line, "Here's my heart, O take and seal it, Seal it for Thy courts above." I pray that my heart is sealed to Jesus, to Spencer, and to my mother.

This may sound strange, but I often strain to try to hear Spencer's voice. The house Vera Mae and I live in now is the house where he died. My favorite room in that house—the room where I like to have meetings, where I go to pray, or sometimes where I just sit—is the room where he used to write. In the black community, our folklore tells us that we're supposed to be afraid to be where somebody died, because their ghost might be there. But I go into that room and sit there at night with the lights off, wishing that Spencer's ghost would appear. I wish that he would talk to me. My daughter Priscilla told me that she does the same thing.

I dream about Spencer too. In the dreams, I'll be spending time with him, having a wonderful time together, but then he always says he has to go. It's like he can't stay with me; he has to go back to where he is now. I wake up from those dreams so sad. It's a little bit like I lose him all over again. But I wouldn't give up those dreams—those few moments when I can see his face and hear his voice again. Until I get to heaven, that's the closest I can be to my beloved son.

Frankly, it is the thought of seeing Spencer and my mother again that keeps me motivated today. I don't expect my mother to be impressed by all my honorary doctorates or the academic centers named after me; rather, I hope she will ask me what I did for mothers like her, mothers dying of nutritional deficiency. And I hope she'll tell me that she was proud that I started health centers and advocated for the WIC program. I hope the choices I have made and the way I have lived my life prove my love for them. But Paul told us in Romans 8 that nothing, including death, can separate us from the greatest love, the love of God, and so I can rest knowing that Spencer, my mother, and I are always resting together in that love.

9

Affirming Human Dignity

I believe in the inherent dignity of all human beings. The Bible states clearly that God created men and women in His image from the very beginning (see Gen. 1:27). No matter how damaged people become, they still bear that image. No matter how much people have been oppressed or how much they have oppressed others, the part of them made in His image is worth rescuing and restoring. Since we all inherently bear this image, we also inherently have dignity. We do not give people dignity; God gives it to them, but we must work to affirm it in others and ourselves.

But I also believe in the fall. I believe we have all fallen short of the righteousness of God. We certainly are in need of redemption, and I'm not saying that dignity is part of a self-help religion where all people are inherently good or could work their way to a perfect state. But Christ came to redeem His people and make them new creations. Through Jesus's death on the cross we were reconciled to God and to one another. And even though we still find ourselves entrapped by sin, we receive by faith the righteousness of God. We have been born again. We still bear His image, and this is a good enough reason to treat every person with dignity.

Evil certainly exists, and when left unchecked, it robs human beings of their dignity. I know firsthand how it feels to be dehumanized, helpless, and hopeless. I know what it feels like to be a target of evil. I felt this most strongly when I was lying in my blood on the floor of the Brandon jail, not able to strike back. But evil isn't always as dramatic as almost dying. There have been other incidents as well, such as the time when I was a teenager and was paid 15 cents for a full day's work. That was an obvious case of one human being devaluing another. I remember the internal struggle I had about how to respond. If I had demanded more money, or even refused to take any money at all, I would have preserved my dignity, but I also would have been branded a little smart-mouth and put myself and my family in danger. I would have been considered too smart, and that would have branded me for further abuse. In that moment, I felt helpless, almost like a victim must feel.

Many years later, a white policeman pulled me over while I was driving a car with some of my children. The officer started picking on me—I know he wanted me to talk back to him so he could arrest me, take me to jail, and perhaps beat me. That was the routine back then. This man mocked me in front of my children. After calling me a racial slur, he asked, "Has the cat got your tongue?" knowing full well I couldn't say a thing to him without being arrested. Despite the words of the First Amendment that declare that there can be no law "abridging the freedom of speech," I was going to be arrested for anything I said. In the officer's eyes, I was not a human, so this right was not granted to me.

Deep inside I struggled with anger, and part of me wanted to lash out at that policeman. But I wasn't going to let him make me hateful, and I refused to take on a victim mentality. So I held my tongue through the insults and waited him out. When the officer was gone, I joked with my children and told them that he needed to treat me that way for his sake. But oppression is no laughing matter. What I've experienced drives me on with a sense of responsibility.

Just before Christmas in 1969, one of our local Mendenhall boys had been beaten by the sheriff for a small offense. This came right on the tail end of another boy being beaten, and I realized we needed to make a stand for freedom. We needed to stand up for our rights, and now there was no turning back. A group of us went to the jail in Mendenhall to protest, but when we did, the police arrested us and put us in jail. Most of the people with me were youth, and so their parents came up to the jail to get them out. I knew this was the time to mobilize my people, so I began giving a speech about standing up for ourselves and fighting for our freedom. I was speaking to the people outside the jail, trying to hold on to my own dignity and inspire them to hold on to theirs as well, but not surprisingly, the white police officers did not want that to happen.

I was trying to get the people of my town to recognize their given rights. The US Declaration of Independence clearly states, "We hold these truths to be self-evident, that all men are created equal, that they are endowed by their Creator with certain unalienable Rights, that among these are Life, Liberty and the pursuit of Happiness." In one of the greatest statements our country has made, the dignity of all human beings is affirmed. It is a disgrace to all people when we don't abide by this.

I understand, though, how people can get trapped into perpetually seeing themselves as victims. It's hard to measure the damage that can be caused by feeling inferior and hopeless. Many oppressed people recoil into survival mode, compromising their dignity and just about everything else just to make it from day to day. But accepting a victim status somehow takes a toll on our physical health. I believe that high blood pressure and a poor diet, coupled with this mind-set as an oppressed people, have created the high percentage of American black men who are dying from hypertension and heart disease.

People should not disconnect their mental state from their physical well-being. Slaves rarely rebelled for many reasons, but one was mere survival. For those born into slavery and who had never tasted freedom, it must have seemed impossible that life could be any different. In order to survive, many felt they had to accept the oppression.

Oftentimes an oppressed people settle into a victim mind-set and accept the oppressor's view of them—that they are of less value than other people, that they don't deserve dignity, and that they don't fully bear the image of God—because it's the easiest thing to do or seems like the only way to survive. They don't realize that physically and psychologically, that kind of outlook is very damaging. Those who fight, survive. Those whose human dignity is not affirmed, and who do not have an avenue to express their dignity, have trouble at every turn, and ultimately many do not survive.

—m—

We all struggle with dignity, even when we know how much God values us. In fact, once we have tasted the promises He has made to us and gotten a glimpse of what we can be, reality can still knock us down. This fact troubles me personally because I saw my own son Spencer wrestle with the reality of his own giftedness. He could play ball with whites, go to college with whites, and graduate with whites, only to realize that in society he was not valued equally as whites with the same credentials. The reality was that he was black—and that fact held him back from accomplishing his dreams.

Spencer was devastated when a couple months before he died, he hurt his leg and the doctors told him he would not be able to play basketball or baseball again. He was a very good athlete, and sports had been his outlet. Spencer also was passionate about racial reconciliation and believed he, his friend Chris Rice, and their team could live it out as well as anyone could. He had the people and felt the pressure to do reconciliation well, but he didn't have enough fiscal resources. When his passion ran head-on into his lack of resources, it weighed him down. Like so many who dream about bettering the world, Spencer knew where he wanted to go, but the path to get there was full of obstacles, some of which were hard to accept and no doubt undercut his dignity.

Success is a big part of nurturing personal worth. While we all cannot be successful at everything, each of us needs to be successful at something. God created us with this need. While we strive for success in our primary passion, which often involves our careers, it helps to have another outlet that affirms the creative dignity given to all of us at birth. For Spencer, that was sports. Once he could no longer compete in sports, his dignity was shaken. Of course, Spencer was a success in other areas of life. He had his family, friends, and faith. But now the spotlight shined even brighter on his passion for reconciliation and the obstacles that were keeping him from being as good at that as he was at sports. I believe that in some ways he died of a broken heart. Some people in my family disagree, but I believe he died because he couldn't see the progress that he had hoped for.

When our source of dignity becomes broken or unavailable, we often feel lost and discouraged. Never give up. We should desire to release and support human dignity in others. We want this dignity to arise and be used for good in the world, for the good of the world.

—⁂—

One way people find dignity is through art. A painter becomes one with his painting. A singer wraps herself up in a song. A writer sits for hours before his computer losing all track of time as he crafts his story. Dignity emerges on a canvas, in a melody, and through words. In August 2010, I was invited to the Greater Philadelphia Christian Writers Conference to speak to some very creative people. I don't consider myself to be a writer, so as I flew into the city that is home to the Liberty Bell and the place where the US Declaration of Independence was signed, I asked God, *What am I doing here?*

My friend Tony Campolo joined me the next day on the platform, and we spoke about the importance of communicating justice issues. If you have ever seen me and Tony together, you know that the room was electrified. We were doing what we love most: helping others catch the vision for reconciliation, compassion, integrity, and freedom for all. As usual, Tony had us all laughing and weeping. Someday I am going to have to ask him how he gets audiences to do both at the same time.

Later in the conference, I was part of a panel that included Geraldine Ryerson-Cruz (a former advocacy writer for World Vision International), Lisa Thompson (formerly of the Salvation Army), and my longtime friend Lisa Sharon Harper (formerly the director of New York Faith and Justice who is now with Sojourners and a member of the Christian Community Development Association). After the session, Lisa Thompson and I talked. At the time, Lisa was the Salvation Army liaison for the abolition of sex trafficking, and she still works to combat trafficking. Human trafficking (which includes sex trafficking) is modern-day slavery—an evil that has grown to be one of the three most lucrative illegal undertakings of our day (along with guns and drugs). As I see it, Lisa is an abolitionist in the spirit of William Wilberforce. So I wanted to hear what she had to say.

"God didn't put anyone on this planet to be a porn star, a prostitute, or a stripper," Lisa said. "Nobody is just a prostitute. Nobody is just a trafficked victim. Each person is somebody's daughter."[1]

Lisa spoke to my heart. She spoke of dignity—God's intended dignity for each of us no matter our past, no matter our present. Each one of us is somebody's son or daughter.

—⁓—

God created all things. He knows the purest expression of our dignity. Because we are made in His image, even in our fallen state we have a sense of creativity and beauty. Conversion and dignity are the realization that we bear God's face—the image of God. Conversion is to turn around when we realize that we are sinners going away from God. Conversion is finding that His love is sufficient for all that we need. We are united with our Maker, and we discover that He gave us the capacity and calling to be creative. Our response to God's love is confidence in who we are in Him. In my teaching, I attribute my calling to hearing His voice. God calls us to find Him, to know Him, to fall in love with Him, and to share His love with others. Love is letting go and allowing God to show us how to express the dignity that He has created in us.

—ɯ—

World Vision International is one of those great organizations that attempts to affirm the dignity of the poor around the world. I had the privilege of serving on the board of directors for eighteen years. When I first joined the board, World Vision was doing wonderful work across the globe. They had implemented some great approaches to relief and development work in needy countries. I, along with other board members—including Roberta Hestenes, Paul Rees, Steve Lazarian, and Colleen Townsend Evans—started talking about economic issues and justice in the United States. I believe we helped World Vision to expand its focus to include holistic development in urban ghettos and rural areas in America. We came to see the importance of affirming the dignity of suffering people in this country as well.

—ɯ—

Dignity has always been part of the justice equation. My ancestors who were slaves wanted it. I wanted it when I was pulled over by the white police officer. Spencer wanted it for himself and his community. How we bring about dignity in the face of oppression has always been a challenge. Taking off the chains, freeing the slaves, and declaring independence is certainly important, but it isn't enough.

So how do we actually bring about dignity?

My friend and CCDA board member Cheryl Miller has learned a lot from both her own experiences and from years of working with formerly addicted, prostituted, or incarcerated women about ways to do this well. In her book *The Language of Shalom*, she tells the story of working with a woman named Sophie in a way that models "compassionate confrontation." Sophie was involved with the Center for Peace, one part of Perpetual Help Home, the nonprofit for which Cheryl is the executive director. The Center for Peace is a social enterprise ministry that helps women gain entrepreneurial skills and develop knowledge of business professionalism in order to help them land jobs or start their own businesses.

The Center for Peace already affirms the dignity of the women working there because it helps give them skills to work, rather than simply allowing them to be the recipients of handouts. However, Cheryl's work with Sophie reveals how to work with people in a way that restores their dignity, rather than allowing them to stay victims. When Sophie wanted to minimize her past, saying she had just made a few mistakes rather than admitting to actually having committed crimes, Cheryl made sure she took full responsibility and accountability for what she had done in her past. However, she did this through a loving relationship that proved she cared. Cheryl even took Sophie back to her hometown and supported her as she made restitution and asked for forgiveness from people she had hurt.

By taking real responsibility, offering a full confession, and receiving true forgiveness, Sophie was able to allow the shame and victimization of her past to fall away and her dignity to be restored.[2]

Nurturing another person's dignity takes creativity, hard work, and love. Yes, there is that word again—*love*. Hymn writer Fanny Crosby summed up the importance of human dignity and the love of God quite well in her 1873 hymn "Blessed Assurance":

> Blessed assurance, Jesus is mine!
> Oh, what a foretaste of glory divine!
> Heir of salvation, purchase of God,
> Born of His Spirit, washed in His blood.

Perfect submission, perfect delight,
Visions of rapture now burst on my sight;
Angels descending, bring from above
Echoes of mercy, whispers of love.

Perfect submission, all is at rest,
I in my Saviour am happy and blest;
Watching and waiting, looking above,
Filled with His goodness, lost in His love.

Refrain:
This is my story, this is my song,
Praising my Saviour all the day long;
This is my story, this is my song,
Praising my Saviour all the day long.[3]

The oppressor and the oppressed reflect a damaged image of God—and long to express their creativity and dignity in a healthy way. For very different reasons, both the oppressed and the oppressors can be hard to love. But Jesus calls us as His followers to love our enemies and also to care for the downtrodden, whether they are in a concentration camp in Germany or in a halfway house in Jackson, Mississippi. Dignity is worth the fight.

10

The Final Fight

Love. No matter where I start, I always end up here.

—⚍—

The birth of my second child, Joanie, was such a happy time because now I had a boy and a girl. When I saw her in Vera Mae's arms, joy swelled up within me. I was consumed by something greater than me.

I can remember one of her early birthdays—we had a big party for her. We invited all of the neighborhood kids and gave each one a balloon. If I close my eyes, I can still picture the scene.

As Joanie grew up, it wasn't all balloons and birthdays. It seemed that she was the most difficult of my children. Perhaps I was a bit difficult too. I always tried to show her love but never felt that I was adequate. As she tumbled into her teen years, she developed a strong-willed mind of her own. Don't ask me where she got that—I know! I only have to look in the mirror.

Our son Phillip came along and became what I call my "knee baby." I probably gave the most time to him, but it was needed because he was sick with polio. No doubt Joanie was slighted. As each child came along, it seemed that there were more needs and less time—and never enough time to catch up with Joanie. There was always an awkward gap between me trying to express my love for her and her receiving it.

Joanie's wedding day was a pinnacle of joy. Naturally, as the father of the bride, I was delighted in the usual ways. At the same time, no one knew it, but I was actually uneasy and conflicted. I wrestled with how disappointed I was in myself for not being able to show her deeper, more tangible love.

As I escorted Joanie down the aisle, so many memories danced through my mind. She was a beautiful woman. I was to give her away to Ron Potter, and I also was to preach a sermon. Several different people were giving talks, and I was to give the last one. But I was so taken by my emotion and tears of joy that I couldn't speak. That was one of only a few times in my life that the emotion of a moment so overwhelmed me. Many feelings rushed through my head and heart, but I knew that Ron would give her love at a depth I never could give her. The genuine joy I felt was indescribable—and still is even all these years later.

Ron has loved and does love Joanie in all the ways she deserves. In many ways, they have a model marriage. It's not perfect, of course, but it's an example to follow. They made the decision to adopt children. Varah was the first. I fell in love with Varah the moment I saw her. There is so much love for her and in her that no one would guess Joanie is not her birth mother. In fact, to me, through love, Varah has become one of us. It was the same with their youngest daughter, Karah. Those two children are the apples of my eye. I love them so dearly.

—⟁—

People ask me to speak about justice, the prisons, race relations, and economic development—and I'm happy to discuss those topics, because I know how important each one is. But I've discovered that I can't talk about any of them for long before love finds its way into the conversation. I have often said that sometimes when I read the Bible, I see justice in every verse. I could say the same about love—maybe even more so.

Looking back—especially at my conversion and early discipleship—I can see how my own need for love, my experience of God's love, and my understanding of the Christian responsibility to love others always undergirded my thinking about life, faith, and ministry. I just didn't always articulate those things as clearly or intentionally as I could have.

God used three key passages of Scripture to start me on my path of walking with Him. The first is Galatians 2:20: "I have been crucified with Christ and I no longer live, but Christ lives in me. The life I now live in the body, I live by faith in the Son of God, who loved me and gave himself for me." This was around the same time that Spencer, who was just three years old, had invited me to attend his Sunday school class. So I went to church because of my love for my son, but what I found there was this amazing idea that God and His Son loved me. It wasn't just a little bit of love we were talking about either. Jesus loved me enough to give His own life for me. As I studied the Scriptures over the next few months, that verse in Galatians spoke to the deepest longing in my life—the desire to experience love that didn't end the way my mother's had ended when she died, and that didn't leave me alone like my father had left me on the railroad tracks when he came to see me for the first time that I can remember. My father had given me to my grandma to care for me after my mother had died when I was seven months old. I could tell that God's love was a great motivating force for Paul, and I wanted to experience it for myself.

So one Sunday morning, the best way I knew how, I asked God to come into my life—and that's when I discovered something fascinating and wonderful about God's love. You see, in that moment, I felt a deep sense of my own sinfulness—my depravity, my emptiness—as well as His deep, forgiving love. I tasted the fear of God. At the same time, though, I was aware of God's presence and met by His grace—it felt like He was putting His arms around me, squeezing me tight, and loving me with His deep, forgiving love. When I felt loved by God, I sensed my own dirtiness and ugliness but knew He was embracing me anyway and His grace was sufficient. When I was fully aware of my sinfulness is when I experienced God's love most fully and couldn't resist Him.

I liken my experience to Paul's experience on the road to Damascus. I can hear in Paul's teaching his sense of God's love. Paul knew Christ in suffering. He felt like he wanted to love God to the point that he would experience suffering like God suffered. Paul saw the depths of God's love for him, and he was willing to suffer for His love. There is some of that in me. I have known His goodness. He has seen me through so much tumult. I'd like to go with Him through even more. So I wonder, *How much do you have for me, God?* Not as a martyr per se, but as one in all that Christ was and is—including the pain. Without the pain, there is no true love. And in some ways, the power of love increases as the suffering is endured. Knowing Christ's pain takes me to a deeper place with Him. The pain of Christ and the forgiveness of our sins are at the core of the gospel.

I did come to see that God *did* know who I was, and He still loved me. He helped me comprehend both my need for a Savior and His willingness to be that Savior for me—to pay the consequences of my sin because of His great love. That experience changed my life forever.

After my profession of faith, an older white man named Wayne Leitch began to disciple me. An artist and theologian, he was the director of Child Evangelism Fellowship in Monrovia, California. He had hope for an elementary school dropout, and he became like a father to me. Out of respect, I called him Mr. Leitch. We talked about many Scripture passages, but three in particular set the course for the rest of my life: Acts 1:8; Galatians 2:20; and 2 Timothy 2:1–2. These three passages have become my life's ministry. Mr. Leitch helped me understand another truth of these passages—we, as Christians, must be stewards of God's love. We are to be Christ's witnesses. We are to share with others what we have received from Him. In other words, our work is to proclaim the message about who Jesus is and what He has done for humanity, including how He loves us so much He was willing to die for us.

As I've continued in my Christian walk, I've come to understand something else about being a witness for Christ: it's not just about telling the story. If we are going to help others understand who Jesus is, our own lives must reflect His character and love. Our lives should bear witness—not primarily to how much we love God but to how much He loves us and how our hearts have been turned because of His deep love for us. Our lives should show that His deep love for us brings us great joy, even in the midst of tribulation. That He would reach down and pick up somebody like me (or like you) and show His love for me and then give me the privilege of sharing that love with others—that's God's miracle. That's incarnation. Jesus was incarnated so we could experience God's love; now we are called to live and minister incarnationally so that others can experience it as well.

The other passage that played an important role in my discipleship comes from Paul's writing, and it has to do with *how* we carry out our mission. Paul instructed his disciple Timothy that "the things you have heard me say in the presence of many witnesses entrust to reliable people who will also be qualified to teach others" (2 Tim. 2:2). This passage instilled in me the importance of developing the local church and raising up indigenous leadership from the community to carry on God's work. No one person is going to carry the gospel to the ends of the earth. The good news about God's love will spread as individuals and small groups of people tell the story and live the reality in front of others who can then do the same.

That's the kind of witness that draws people in. Sadly, when many look at the church in America today, they don't see a group of disciples characterized by love for one another. Instead, they see (and hear) a group of people making a lot of noise about issues—abortion, homosexuality, and other social and political hot topics. It's not that those things aren't important—they are very important, and Christians are right to raise issues and take stands. But those things shouldn't define the church. Human personalities shouldn't define the church, either. Our Christianity should be defined by Christ—who loved us and gave His earthly life for us—living His everlasting life out through us.

I like the way A. W. Tozer writes about Jesus's sacrificial love:

What brought Jesus Christ to die? "Thou visitest him," the Scriptures record. Why did he visit us? Was it that he might carry out the eternal purpose? Yes, but that is not the way to look at it. He visited us because we were a fixture in his mind. He came for us as a mother wakes in the morning and runs into the room to see if the baby is all right. It was love that brought him down to die. God's anxious, restless love was incarnated in human flesh. This accounts for the character of Christ and for his attitude toward people and his tireless labor for them. This ultimately accounts for his dying for them at last. . . .

Our Lord's great pain for us compelled him to come down to earth. Calvary was a pain. . . . The nails were painful. And the hanging there, perspiring in the hot sun with the flies, must have been a painful, awful experience. But one pain was bigger than the other. It was the bigger pain that drove him to endure the little pain. And the smaller pain was his pain of dying. The greater pain was his pain of loving. . . . To love and not be loved in return is one of the most exquisite pains in the entire repertoire of painfulness. So He came, He lived, He loved, and He died and death could not destroy that love. It is still a fixture in His mind.[1]

God loved us so much—He was so pained by our separation from Him and our rejection of Him—that He was willing to endure both the day-to-day pains of human existence and the excruciating physical pain of death on the cross. That's a depth of love that I can only barely begin to comprehend, but as much as I can understand it, I am amazed by and grateful for it.

In studying John 3:16, "For God so loved the world that he gave his one and only Son, that whoever believes in him shall not perish but have eternal life," I've come to see this verse as the centerpiece of the New Testament. I think the most important thing we can know about God is how much He loves us and wants us to be part of His family—and how the way for that to happen is through Christ, not our own striving. So becoming a Christian is discovering God's love for us, and being a Christian is learning to love God back—and then finding ways to show God's overflowing love to the people around us. Or, as John writes:

Dear friends, let us love one another, for love comes from God. Everyone who loves has been born of God and knows God. Whoever does not love does not know God, because God is love. This is how God showed his love among us: He sent his one and only Son into the world that we might live through him. This is love: not that we loved God, but that he loved us and sent his Son as an atoning sacrifice for our sins. Dear friends, since God so loved us, we also ought to love one another. (1 John 4:7–11)

John emphasizes that love begins with God. We experience God's love first, and then we are able to truly love others. It's tempting for us to claim that our love and our good works start with us. But really, the more we receive Christ's love and the more we worship God in gratitude for the love He's shown us, the more we are motivated to show love and do good works.

Sometimes we look at the Bible and think that the Old Testament is about the law, and the New Testament is about love, but in fact, the central truth of the Old Testament is that God loved Abraham, Isaac, Jacob, and their descendants. He formed them into a nation, redeemed that nation from slavery, and brought them into a good land to inhabit. Even though they often rebelled, and God had to discipline them, He always brought them back. He never stopped loving them; they remained "a fixture in His mind."

He loves us all with a divine purpose. He loved Abraham because He had a divine purpose. Deuteronomy 7:9 says, "Know therefore that the LORD your God is God; he is the faithful God, keeping his covenant of love to a thousand generations of those who love him and keep his commandments." Everyone who came after the Israelites would know that He would carry out His love for them too. That covenant love is exemplary of His love—a love that endures. The Old Testament was a prototype that He was holding up for all of humanity. He was going to then send all those who accepted, cherished, and embraced that love into the world to share the good news. The church is the vehicle for spreading that good news.

Israel's story reveals a great deal about God's love for us today—how He sent Jesus to redeem us from slavery to sin and how He remains faithful and committed to us even when we fall short in our obedience to—and love for—Him.

God's love isn't the only thing that helps develop our ability to show compassion and do good in the world—the love of other people does that for us as well. We're involved in God's work in one another. When I was a new Christian, one of the ways God taught me about His love for me was through Mr. Leitch, who met my hunger to know God by discipling me in the study of the Bible. He also affirmed what he saw God doing in me and preparing me for. When I had just started teaching—when I was still overcoming my stutter and feeling inadequate for the ministry God seemed to be calling me to—Mr. Leitch told me that he believed that one day people all over the world would ask me to come and share the gospel in their communities. I doubted him. But God used this older brother in the Lord to rid me of my unbelief—to help me see what He could do in my life. He gave me hope. He used Mr. Leitch as part of His redemptive process in my life.

God too had to rid the apostle Paul (who was once known as Saul) of his unbelief. He had an amazing encounter with Jesus on the road to Damascus. After striking down Paul, God asked, "Saul, Saul, why do you persecute me?" (Acts 9:4), but I think His underlying message was "Saul, I love you. Why don't you love Me?" Jesus could have taken care of everything right there. He could have sent him on his mission to the gentiles immediately. But He didn't. Instead, He sent Paul into the city and used a man named Ananias to be an instrument of His love in Saul's life. Ananias came offering forgiveness, healing, and fellowship to this Pharisee who had been persecuting believers. Jesus's intervention in Saul's life—His meeting him personally—was the greatest love Saul could or would ever know.

When we love others in the name of Christ—even if they have wronged us in the past and even if showing our love makes us vulnerable to the possibility that they will harm us again—we participate in God's redemptive work in their lives. Both Paul and Peter acknowledged love's power in their epistles. Paul counseled married believers not to leave spouses who didn't know Christ, because "how do you know, wife, whether you will save your husband? Or, how do you know, husband, whether you will save your wife?" (1 Cor. 7:16). Similarly, Peter exhorted wives to "submit yourselves to your own husbands so that, if any of them do not believe the word, they may be won over without words by the behavior of their wives, when they see the purity and reverence of your lives" (1 Pet. 3:1–2).

These apostles understood that devotion and loving obedience have the potential to draw people to Christ. When we come to know Christ, we have a responsibility to so love others that they may also recognize Christ's redemptive power and great love for them. Of course, there's no guarantee someone will change just because we love them, but there is power in deep and sincere love.

—✠—

I speak often about the ways that we black men have let down our women, children, and communities. Fatherlessness is an epidemic today, and my heart is broken for the women, and especially the children, who have been abandoned, so I plead with men to take responsibility and love their families.

Sometimes when I address this subject, women ask me what they can do to confront this failure in our men and strengthen our families and communities. I tell my sisters that, as hurt and disappointed as they may be, the way to bring our men back is to show them deep love as human beings created by God in His image and with inherent dignity. I understand that this is not an easy thing to do, but God calls us to love the people who have hurt us—just as Jesus loved Saul who was persecuting Him. Jesus used strong language to make a statement about loving those who are hard for us to love:

> You have heard that it was said, "Love your neighbor and hate your enemy." But I tell you, love your enemies and pray for those who persecute you, that you may be children of your Father in heaven. He causes his sun to rise on the evil and the good, and sends rain on the righteous and the unrighteous. If you love those who love you, what reward will you get? Are not even the tax collectors doing that? (Matt. 5:43–46)

Love is most powerful when it is unexpected—and when it does not come cheaply. God's love for us is certainly like that. We have not earned it, and it comes at the highest cost: "But God demonstrates his own love for us in this: While we were still sinners, Christ died for us" (Rom. 5:8). In the same way, we are called to love those who sin against us, even if we must sacrifice something to do so.

When asked what God's greatest commandment is, Jesus answered, "'Love the Lord your God with all your heart and with all your soul and with all your mind.' This is the first and greatest commandment. And the second is like it: 'Love your neighbor as yourself.' All the Law and the Prophets hang on these two commandments" (Matt. 22:37–40). In Luke's version of this teaching, Jesus illustrates the second commandment by telling the parable of the good Samaritan—a story in which two religious leaders ignore a neighbor in need, while a Samaritan gives his time and money to help someone whom he most likely would have considered his enemy (see Luke 10:25–37). The Samaritan could have felt justified in leaving an injured Jew in a ditch—according to human standards, he didn't have any obligation to help someone who probably wouldn't have helped him if their situations had been reversed. But he showed love and mercy to this stranger—to this enemy. When He finished telling the story, Jesus said, "Go and do likewise" (Luke 10:37).

Now, I've noticed something interesting about my "enemies" as I've gone through life: I often learn from them. Many times, when people cut me down, there's some bit of truth in what they say—and if I can hear that truth, I may be able to grow and do better in my service to God. When that happens, I'm grateful for my enemies. Maybe I even love them a little bit for helping me become a better Christian. Jesus may have had that idea in His mind when He told us to love our enemies, but I think mostly He just meant for us to do it, whether or not we see any benefit in it. The real advantage for us, of course, is that the more we practice loving the people who are hard for us to love, the more we reflect Jesus's character and build our "grace muscles" so we can respond in an even more Christlike manner the next time.

I've understood from early on in my Christian walk that God commands us to love all people, and I've known that God has called me to be a reconciler, but I've still struggled to love some people. I've had nightmares about Lloyd "Goon" Jones and the other highway patrol officers who beat me and the Tougaloo College students in jail, and learning to love them has not come easy. Judge Cox is another one. He was a federal judge who always ruled against blacks. That was his way of dispensing justice. Judge Cox was the federal judge presiding when we were suing to move the case surrounding our beating to the federal court. He treated us like dogs in the courthouse, eventually ruling against us.

We appealed and moved it up to the fifth circuit court that also ruled against us. We were getting ready to take it to the Supreme

Court, but our lawyers encouraged us to settle. The attorneys decided if they dropped the charges against us, we should drop the charges against them, so that became the settlement.

Goon Jones was the highway inspector who led the beating in the jail. He was also the officer who led the May 15, 1970, shooting at a girls' dormitory at Jackson State University (JSU). In the wake of the Kent State University protests and in objection to the racial harassment that often took place at JSU, a historically black university, students initiated their own set of demonstrations beginning on Thursday, May 14. The student/police action culminated in officers shooting up a girls' dormitory shortly after midnight on Friday, killing two people and wounding twelve others.[2]

On the same day as the JSU demonstrations, Connie Slaughter, one of my attorneys, had taken Goon Jones's deposition in regard to my case. She had the chance to cross-examine him. In many ways, the shooting probably seemed like payback for him. Having a black woman ask him all those questions and accuse him of lying—it was basically unthinkable at the time, and the shootings at JSU probably seemed like an opportunity for him to once again assert his dominance and place in society.

Goon Jones retired from the state highway patrol to run for Simpson County sheriff, a position he held for nineteen years. He beat us up, and it made him more popular. In 1995, Jones and a jail trusty were shot and killed by a black man in Jones's front yard. When Jones died, my daughter Elizabeth asked Vera Mae how she should feel that the man who had beat her daddy had been killed. Vera Mae said to Elizabeth, "The Bible says, 'You live by the sword, you die by the sword.'" (See Rev. 13:10.) Goon Jones was arrogant too, and that makes it harder. When someone acts in humility—when there's some sign of repentance for their harmful actions—forgiving them is more tolerable. But when a person displays a haughty mind-set—well, it's really hard to show them love.

I know I'm not the only Christian who sometimes has a hard time loving my enemies. A recent nationwide Barna Group study looked at positive and negative contributions that Christianity has made in society. On the negative side, this is what they found: "When asked to identify what they thought were the negative contributions of Christians to American society in recent years, the most frequent response was violence or hatred incited in the name of Jesus Christ. One out of five Americans mentioned such vitriolic attitudes." On the positive side, "One out of every five adults (19 percent) mentioned how Christians in the United States have helped poor or underprivileged people to have a better life."[3]

Of course, that positive statement thrills me. But the two taken together remind me of something the apostle Paul wrote: "If I give all I possess to the poor and give over my body to hardship that I may boast, but do not have love, I gain nothing" (1 Cor. 13:3). We as Christians are called to be recognized as Jesus's disciples by the love we show to others—instead, we're known for our hatred. This is tragic—and dangerous. Consider John's teaching on this subject: "Whoever claims to love God yet hates a brother or sister is a liar. For whoever does not love their brother and sister, whom they have seen, cannot love God, whom they have not seen" (1 John 4:20).

When I think about loving people who are hard to love, my mind often returns to Saul and Ananias. Paul called himself the worst of sinners (see 1 Tim. 1:15), and his actions before he encountered Christ really were horrific. He approved of the murder of Stephen—and on the same day, a persecution started in which "Saul began to destroy the church" (Acts 8:3). As believers fled Jerusalem, Saul continued "breathing out murderous threats against the Lord's disciples. He went to the high priest and asked him for letters to the synagogues in Damascus, so that if he found any there who belonged to the Way, whether men or women, he might take them as prisoners to Jerusalem" (Acts 9:1–2).

I wonder what I would have done if God had instructed me, as He did Ananias, to minister to this man. What would you have done? What would I do today if God told me He was doing redemptive work in the hearts of the leaders of al-Qaida or ISIS—and He wanted me to be a part of it? Could I love someone who had been committed to destroying people like me? Come to think of it, am I praying, even now, that God *will* get hold of their hearts? Am I praying that they will have transformational encounters with Christ that will completely turn their lives around? (Did I ever pray for Osama bin Laden in that way?) What would my reaction be if the 9/11 masterminds sent out a new video saying that Jesus had visited them like He visited Saul? Would I go to them, ready to provide whatever healing and encouragement they needed so they could begin to dedicate their lives to the cause of Christ? If they turned themselves in, they would still need to face the consequences of their actions.

My forgiving al-Qaida and God forgiving them would not remove the government's responsibility to bring them to trial for the murders they have committed. Honestly, I probably would find it very hard to forgive them, considering they murdered nearly three thousand people on September 11 and many others throughout the years across the globe.

It seems to me that we have a limited and distorted idea of love. Somehow we've developed the mind-set that to love one person or group, we have to hate another person or group. So we direct our love toward the groups we're part of—our families, our denominations, our political parties, our ethnic groups—and feel free to hate anyone outside of these boxes. We may not hate them individually, but we hate them collectively. We condemn people for not belonging to the same groups we belong to—we look down on them for not thinking like us, worshiping like us, voting like us, or looking like us. Maybe we justify this behavior because we think the other group is wrong about God. Jesus doesn't let us get away with that though. He taught that even being angry with someone else was

152

like murder—and it made the angry person subject to judgment (see Matt. 5:21–22).

—◊◊◊—

As a reconciler, I find myself interacting with people on all parts of the political spectrum. I tend to get in a little trouble with all of them from time to time, but I'm willing to risk offending people if it will help all of us to love better. One area that causes some tension—including at CCDA, where there's a great deal of political diversity—is the pro-life debate. Some liberals get nervous when I say I'm pro-life. For the most part, I think they're reacting to the right-wing idea of pro-life, which sometimes seems interested in only certain kinds of lives—unborn children, for instance. I am extremely interested in the rights of the unborn, but my passion for life does not stop when a baby emerges from his or her mother's womb. I believe God wants us to be concerned for every life, including the lives of our young black men in jail, Mexican immigrants (legal or not) living in America, gay men and women, and so many others—saints and sinners!

A while back I gave a talk at an immigration rally in Phoenix. I told the people there that I didn't come to talk about the legal questions—I don't know enough about that aspect of the issue to speak on it. I just came because I wanted to be with my neighbors. I wanted to say to my neighbors on both sides of the US border that I love them. When I think about borders, what often comes to mind is Jesus and His family going to Egypt to escape Herod's persecution.

Can you imagine how different things might have been if Jesus hadn't been allowed across into Egypt? He took refuge in a foreign land until it was safe for Him to return to His home country. I don't know how to translate that into immigration policy, but I know it says something to us about neighbors and borders. It is the government's responsibility to monitor and manage its borders, but that has nothing to do with me loving my neighbors on both sides. I give the state the responsibility of managing immigration, and I take responsibility for showing love.

According to that recent Barna Group survey I already mentioned, the second most frequent response in the negative contribution category was "the opposition of Christians to gay marriage."[4] I personally am not in favor of gay marriage. However, I think it is significant that the way in which Christians have approached this issue is viewed as a negative contribution to society. So much hatred finds its way into discussions about this issue, and I often feel the need to apologize to the gay and lesbian community for the church's inability to find the right language to affirm gay people as human beings. Yes, people have different opinions and beliefs about this topic, but there must be a way to discuss it *and* demonstrate love at the same time.

—∙∙—

Another hot-button issue is gentrification, which takes place when urban developers come into dilapidated, urban neighborhoods, fix up the houses, bring in new businesses, and up the property values in the neighborhood.

Clearly, the revitalization of neighborhoods that were once run-down or abandoned is a good thing, but too often upper- and middle-class folks move into these neighborhoods, displacing low-income families and pushing out existing businesses. Instead, what we need to see is development that is centered on love and looks first to the people already living in an area and works with them to develop their neighborhood. New businesses can provide job opportunities for people who used to have to drive far away to find work and can instill hope in people who have been stuck in cycles of poverty. Through such collaboration, thriving multiethnic, multiclass neighborhoods can result rather than segregated neighborhoods at the expense of poor minorities.

In my own hometown of Jackson, Mississippi, I have been encouraged to see some of this type of development happening. I have seen it, for example, in the Fondren and Belhaven neighborhoods, where Belhaven University, my son Spencer's alma mater, is located. During segregation, Belhaven was an entirely white neighborhood. When segregation became illegal, the same thing happened in Jackson that happened all over the country: the white people fled to the suburbs as black people started moving in. However, in Belhaven, things were different. Because the college was there along with a prominent church, many wealthier white people chose to stay despite changing neighborhood dynamics. It definitely took some stretching, but I watched Belhaven University (Belhaven College at the time) welcome my Spencer and learn to embrace him. Today the school is probably one of the most diverse private Christian schools in the nation, with students from thirty countries.

As a result, the Belhaven neighborhood has become fairly diverse itself, and when I go there to eat lunch or spend time in the businesses, I see blacks and whites working and eating together. It's a comfortable multiethnic environment.

However, I don't want to pretend that Belhaven is without problems. In 2015, an older white woman was murdered by younger African American men who robbed her, and my heart aches at the thought of what her family has felt and the fear her neighbors have experienced. It is my hope, though, that the Belhaven community will not be subject to the same fate as so many other urban communities. Even as more gentrification occurs in Jackson, I don't worry as much that the minorities of Belhaven will get pushed out. I see the people of that neighborhood acting in love toward one another. I pray they will continue to come around each other in the love they have often displayed, embracing their neighbors who are different, comforting the ones who are mourning, and caring for one another the way a community should.

Love like that might look pretty strange to the world—but it would surely get people's attention. I think it would get God's attention too. Many people might get angry, but it would also make them ask about this God who commands His people to love in that way—because He first loved them. Love like that would certainly be compelling.

—∿—

When I talk about love being the final fight, sometimes people are confused about what that means. When we think about fighting, we usually think about inflicting physical or emotional harm on one another—we punch, we shoot, we yell—we are violent. When we think about love, we get an entirely different picture in our minds—we think of gentleness, perhaps, or romance or kindness. So what does this love fight look like? One thing that's important to understand is the biblical definition of love. John describes love this way:

> This is how we know what love is: Jesus Christ laid down his life for us. And we ought to lay down our lives for our brothers and sisters. If anyone has material possessions and sees a brother or sister in need but has no pity on them, how can the love of God be in that person? Dear children, let us not love with words or tongue but with actions and in truth. (1 John 3:16–18)

Love is action; it is truth; and it is sacrifice. Love is being willing to give our lives for and to one another. It is sharing what God has given us—whether that means material possessions, wisdom, or anything else He has entrusted to our stewardship.

Inside and outside the church, we've missed this. Liberals, conservatives, Christians, Jews, and Muslims—we've missed a genuine understanding of God's message. It is, very simply, His love for us, and the power He gives us to love one another. Jesus willingly died for people who mocked and rejected Him. He loved them that much—and He fought for their salvation. He fought not by inflicting violence on those who sought to harm Him but by submitting Himself to violence in order to bring about redemption for those He loved.

My most unshakeable belief is in God and His love for me. Whatever else I think I know, I am certain that He loves me, and I believe

Paul's statement that "neither death nor life, neither angels nor demons, neither the present nor the future, nor any powers, neither height nor depth, nor anything else in all creation, will be able to separate us from the love of God that is in Christ Jesus our Lord" (Rom. 8:38–39). Because I am convinced of that love, I am committed to spending the rest of my life fighting the good fight by being a conduit of God's love to those who desperately need to experience it.

Love was my first fight, and Lord willing, it will also be my last. It is my prayer that CCDA and all the organizations around the country that have been influenced by these ideas will continue this fight.

11

The Power of Forgiveness

I've returned many times over the years to the spot in New Hebron where my brother Clyde was shot. Early on, as I stood in that place, all the emotions of that day would come rushing back to me—the pain, the fear, the confusion, the anger.

Recently when I went back, some sixty-two years after Clyde's death, I was surprised to notice that I didn't feel any of those things anymore. I remembered them, sure, but I didn't feel them. I have to admit, that shocked me a little bit. As I stood there, I reflected on all God has done in my life since that terrible day. I remembered how Clyde's killing was, in a way, what got me out of Mississippi. It drove me to California, where I came to know Jesus and heard God's call to ministry. This tragedy contributed to who I've become, and that reveals the grace of redemption. It still amazes me the way God takes truly awful things that happen and uses them for His good purposes.

Until that recent visit I guess I hadn't realized that my forgiveness of the man who killed my brother—and the people who maintained the system of injustice that made that killing not only possible but also permissible—was so complete. Any hatred I had harbored toward them was gone. Of course, most of those people are gone too, so they'll never know that I've forgiven them. But that's okay. My forgiveness of those people is God's gracious gift to me. Forgiving has healed me and set me free.

During that visit I saw both blacks and whites lining the street together, waiting for a Christmas parade to start. The health center we started is still there, serving the community. I rejoice about those things.

To build a system that accommodates the oppression of anyone is wrong. Frederick Douglass said there isn't a single attribute of God, not a single thought, which would accommodate the oppression of another. How can you oppress a brother or sister and call yourself a child of God? To put it another way, "Anyone who hates a brother or sister is in the darkness and walks around in the darkness. They do not know where they are going, because the darkness has blinded them" (1 John 2:11). Those who exercise hatred and oppression have distanced themselves from God and are in a position of grave need.

Of course, it's not always easy to see oppressors as needing our love and compassion. Corrie ten Boom was a Christian in the Netherlands who, along with her family, helped Jews escape the Holocaust during World War II before they were imprisoned by the Nazis. Corrie and her sister were prisoners at the extermination camp called Ravensbrück. In her memoir *The Hiding Place*, she describes the moment when she first thought of her oppressors as people who needed compassion. This conversation took place just after a mentally handicapped girl was brutally beaten by one of the guards:

> "Betsie," I whispered when The Snake was far enough away, "what can we do for these people? Afterward I mean. Can't we make a home for them and care for them and love them?"
>
> "Corrie, I pray every day that we will be allowed to do this! To show them that love is greater!"

160

And it wasn't until I was gathering twigs later in the morning that I realized that I had been thinking of the feeble-minded, and Betsie of their persecutors.[1]

The heart of God's love is forgiveness. It is in His nature to forgive, for He is a merciful God. David knew that because he writes, "When we were overwhelmed by sins, you forgave our transgressions" (Ps. 65:3), and "The LORD is compassionate and gracious, slow to anger, abounding in love. . . . He does not treat us as our sins deserve or repay us according to our iniquities" (Ps. 103:8, 10). Paul knew it too: "For he has rescued us from the dominion of darkness and brought us into the kingdom of the Son he loves, in whom we have redemption, the forgiveness of sins" (Col. 1:13–14). So did Peter: "Repent, then, and turn to God, so that your sins may be wiped out, that times of refreshing may come from the Lord, and that he may send the Messiah, who has been appointed for you—even Jesus" (Acts 3:19–20).

I mention these three men specifically because they illustrate so well an important biblical idea: God uses the weak and sinful to show His power and strength. David committed adultery with Bathsheba and sent Uriah into a situation where he would almost certainly be killed. Paul was, at minimum, an accessory to murder and a persecutor of Christians. Peter denied Christ before His crucifixion. Yet God called David a man after His own heart, established David as king over Israel, and incarnated Himself in the world as one of David's descendants. God turned Paul and Peter into the two greatest leaders in the New Testament church. His ability to use these individuals didn't depend on their being perfect—it depended only on their being forgiven. I don't claim to know all the reasons for God's choice to use such broken people to do His work in the world. I do know that His doing so makes it clear that the power comes from Him and not from the human beings who serve Him.

I also know that God's history of choosing and using damaged men and women gives me hope. It should give all of us hope. If

God could and would forgive, heal, empower, and bless these sinful human beings, can't we trust that He is ready and eager to do the same for us? I'm tremendously thankful to know and serve a God who is merciful—who doesn't hold our failures over our heads but instead binds up our wounds, cleanses us of our iniquity, and allows us to participate in His great plan.

The stories of David, Paul, and Peter bring to mind another biblical principle: the more we've been forgiven, the more we love (see Luke 7:36–50). The greater our experience of God's forgiveness for our sins against Him, the more devoted we are going to be to Him. Likewise, the more we experience mercy from our brothers and sisters, the more we will love them. So forgiveness has power both for the forgiver and for the forgiven. Experiencing forgiveness in either direction provides a wonderful release from bondage—whether that bondage is to bitterness or guilt. I'm sure that's why God instructed us both to forgive and to ask for forgiveness in the Lord's Prayer (see Matt. 6:9–13).

There's a part of the Lord's Prayer that can be both terrifying and liberating if we take it seriously. "'Forgive us our debts, as we also have forgiven our debtors. And lead us not into temptation, but deliver us from the evil one.' For if you forgive other people when they sin against you, your heavenly Father will also forgive you. But if you do not forgive others their sins, your Father will not forgive your sins" (Matt. 6:12–15). So many of us struggle to forgive those who have sinned against us. Because of that, these can be frightening verses. But I think this is a hopeful message. The point here is that we can have our sins forgiven, and we can forgive others. The fact that we ought to forgive others is a burden. The fact that we can forgive others is a blessing.

As Christians, we must talk about evil, sin, and darkness. I am convinced that racism and all the other "-isms"—tribalism, sexism, classism, and others—that keep people apart are evil. The first sin of Adam and Eve separated human beings from God and from one another. Anything that widens that divide is also sin—it contradicts God's will for humans as a community and for each of us individually. It's total rebellion against the gospel, which bridges the gap between human beings and God, and between one human being and another. So we must talk about these things. But as we do so, we need to lower our hostile voices. We need to ask ourselves some hard questions. We need to ask, "Is it judgment or love that brings light into dark places?"

One thing my experience with sin has taught me is that it makes victims of both the oppressed and the oppressor. Both are bound by unforgiveness. Forgiveness finally breaks through our rejection and prepares our deepest emotions to align with the will of God, telling God that we need Him and that we cannot forgive in and of ourselves. It's our yielding to God, rather than to temptation. In forgiveness I recognize that I, John Perkins, have a problem, and God's power is needed to fix it. Since God knows all, my confession of sin affirms the deity of God, and all the attributes of God. What's needed then is a benediction:

> Now may the God of peace—
>   who brought up from the dead our Lord Jesus,
> the great Shepherd of the sheep,
>   and ratified an eternal covenant with his blood—
> may he equip you with all you need
>   for doing his will.
> May he produce in you,
>   through the power of Jesus Christ,
> every good thing that is pleasing to him.
>   All glory to him forever and ever! Amen. (Heb. 13:20–21 NLT)

—᛫ᚻ᛫—

Many people complain these days about how our culture is rabid about scandal, and I don't blame them. It's unfortunate that there are people out there—whether enemies or opportunists—who are eager to bring up the past sins of others and use them to cause trouble. That is cruel and ungodly behavior. But there is a flip side to this coin. With the internet and twenty-four-hour news stations and all the other ways to share information almost immediately, it's difficult to keep our transgressions a secret anymore. Transparency—this understanding that it's getting harder and harder to hide anything—could make us more likely to seek and extend forgiveness. After all, that is what God commands us to do: "Therefore confess your sins to each other and pray for each other so that you may be healed" (James 5:16).

This brings us to another key piece of the forgiveness puzzle, and that is repentance. Repentance is the gateway to God's grace; it is the only way out of our sinful condition. Peter exhorted the crowd at Pentecost, "Repent and be baptized, every one of you, in the name of Jesus Christ for the forgiveness of your sins. And you will receive the gift of the Holy Spirit" (Acts 2:38). John assures us that "if we confess our sins, he is faithful and just and will forgive us our sins and purify us from all unrighteousness" (1 John 1:9). And way back in the Old Testament, God promised Solomon, "If my people, who are called by my name, will humble themselves and pray and seek my face and turn from their wicked ways, then I will hear from heaven, and I will forgive their sin and will heal their land" (2 Chron. 7:14).

I had the privilege of being friends with the late Frank Pollard. Dr. Pollard was the senior pastor at First Baptist Church in Jackson during the 1970s. In 1979, *Time* magazine selected him as one of America's most outstanding Protestant preachers—and he was an outstanding preacher. Dr. Pollard would have liked to allow blacks to attend his church, but most of his deacons wouldn't have allowed it. He left First Baptist in 1980 to serve as the president of Golden Gate Baptist Seminary near San Francisco, only to return in 1986, at a time when blacks were now accepted. However, it wasn't until November 1998 that any black preacher spoke from First Baptist's pulpit on a Sunday morning. Prior to that, another black preacher spoke at a Sunday evening service during a conference.

Dr. Pollard and I were regarded as senior statesmen of sorts, and we did several workshops together from time to time. At one of these workshops, after he had retired from pastoring at First Baptist, he said to me, "One of my greatest regrets is that I never had you at the church to preach." He told me this with such deep sadness, as if he realized that God had called him to do something, and he hadn't done it. That's one of the saddest things in life—to recognize a missed opportunity to be obedient to God. I was grateful that Dr. Pollard said what he said—not because I had felt bad about not getting to speak at his church, but because I knew he needed to know that he was forgiven. I certainly understood how he had felt trapped by the culture he was in, and I didn't want his heart to be heavy anymore because of this thing he hadn't done. I was glad to have that chance to tell him that I forgave him for that—and I know God forgave him for it too.

That moment between Dr. Pollard and me was very personal. At the gala in June 2010 to celebrate my and Vera Mae's fifty-nine years of marriage and fifty years of ministry, another distinguished white Mississippi man offered a more public confession. That man was former Mississippi Governor William Winter. Before I share with you some of the things he said that night, let me give you a little background about our relationship.

I first met Governor Winter back in 1967—only he wasn't the governor yet. He ran for that office the first time in 1967 and lost in the primaries against a man named John Bell Williams. Williams had been in the US House of Representatives. He won as a Democrat but then endorsed a Republican's bid for president, so his own party eventually stripped him of his party leadership role. Anyway, he came back to Mississippi and ran for governor. In his campaign, Williams painted Winter as a superliberal who was going to turn the state over to blacks. Winter was friendly to the black community—and he wasn't willing to reject us to try to win the election, so of course he lost. He ran again in 1979 and won. That was the year that the second health clinic, this one in New Hebron, was opened. Governor Winter was invited to speak at the dedication.

Governor Winter and I were honored together ten years after my beating in the Rankin County Jail in Brandon for our reconciliation work in Mississippi. We were honored together again in 2010 by Mission Mississippi for Reconciliation Month in the state of Mississippi.

A lot of the elderly in the community, both black and white, came out for the dedication, and they just loved Governor Winter. He went around and shook everybody's hands, and they were in awe of him. During his time in office, he showed tremendous concern for education, pushing for the Mississippi Education Reform Act of 1982, which got passed. That was the first time statewide public kindergarten was mandated for every school district in Mississippi. A couple of years after the New Hebron clinic opened, we started another one in Jackson and invited Governor Winter to dedicate that health center as well.

At the dedication he asked me, "John, if you were the governor, what would you do for Mississippi?"

I told him, "I'd spend some time up in the Delta, going around and talking to people. I'd tell them what government couldn't do for them. I'd talk to them about what we, the government, could do together with them. I'd use my governorship to give hope to people in these towns and try to motivate them to do their part to improve their situations." Well, shortly after that conversation, I read in the paper that William Winter was planning to spend a week in the Delta!

My family moved out to Pasadena the next year, but when we returned in 1996, I invited Governor Winter over to our house, and after that we began to get invited to participate in various events together to speak about reconciliation. He served on President Clinton's Advisory Board on Race around that time, and in 1999 he founded the William Winter Institute for Racial Reconciliation at the University of Mississippi. Winter and I had always gotten along well and respected each other's work. Still, I wasn't expecting the words he spoke at our anniversary celebration. Rather than try to explain what he said, I'd like to share these excerpts with you:

I don't have to remind you of what Mississippi was like in the '40s and '50s and '60s. I remember those years, as many of you do. Those years when this man was beaten and almost killed, and his brother was killed, just a few miles from where we have gathered tonight. Why? Simply because of what they look like. Simply because they were African American.

We hear a lot about terrorism these days, but let me tell you something: Mississippi had its share of terrorists back when John Perkins first came along. But he did not let them destroy him or his commitment as a Christian to stand up for right and justice. He possessed those special qualities of leadership that gave him the vision to transform what is into what ought to be. Not what ought to be just for ourselves, but what ought to be better for all of us.

A free society cannot exist for long if too many people in that society put their own image above that of their community. So if we really love our country, we don't have a choice but to work, to serve our neighbors—especially our less fortunate neighbors—and to build up the community in which we live.

That is the only way our system can survive. And that is a lesson I think that John and Vera Mae Perkins have taught us; I know they have taught me. They have been an inspiration for me. I would say to them that wherever black people were enslaved for a long time—both literally and by a system of racial apartheid or racial segregation—we white folks were also prisoners of that system. I would say to you, John and Vera Mae, when you did so much to help break that old system—to help free black people from it—you freed me as well.

And one of the regrets that I have is that I didn't have as much courage as I should have had to openly and visibly support you in those early efforts, and I apologize. I apologize to all of the African Americans in this gathering tonight and in this community and in this state for that dereliction of not having gotten out in the frontlines.

But I also express my gratitude for enabling me to live a freer, more open, more rewarding, and more fulfilling life because of your breaking up that closed society.

Whether we recognize it or not, whether we want to accept it or not, all of us in this country are party to a contract that was entered into a long time ago. And that contract was expressed in the words of the Declaration of Independence where we pledged to each other our lives, our fortunes, and our sacred honor. Those words bind us today just as surely as they bound the people who wrote them. And if anything, their significance is greater now than it was then because the world is smaller now, and it's more dangerous now. The issues are more complex; the stakes are higher.

All of this simply means that we cannot live in isolation from each other. And we must find more ways to give real meaning to that contract that we have with each other. As never before in our history, we are called upon to sustain and expand our commitment to build up the communities where we live. Here in the Jackson metropolitan area and all of Mississippi, as far as we have come, we have to understand how much more we still have to do. For unless we continue to work, to breach the fault lines of race and class and financial disparity that still divide us, we can never expect to reach our true potential as a state and as a nation. These problems weigh especially heavily on us here in Mississippi because of our past mistakes that I've referred to—because we deferred for so long putting into effect the terms of that contract.

And all of us have to be involved in solving those problems now and solving them together.[2]

Confession is powerful. It has power in it. It has erasing power.

I was absolutely blown away by my friend's words. They reminded me of what Dr. Martin Luther King Jr. said: "injustice anywhere is a threat to justice everywhere."[3] Mr. Winter also reminded me of what God had taught me back in Brandon—that racism enslaves the oppressor as well as the oppressed. To hear not just a white man, but a former governor of Mississippi, acknowledge those truths and apologize to me and African Americans everywhere was pretty amazing. It was a healing moment, and it gave me hope that maybe someday we will see something like that on a national level (not that the apology would be directed at me, of course, but just that there could be a national acknowledgment of the sin of racism that has stained our nation's history).

A few people have tried to offer such apologies. Different white Christian groups have sponsored national days of repentance in Washington—I've been to a few of those. Some politicians have made an effort too. Tony Hall, who served as a Democratic congressman from Ohio for more than twenty years, and Duncan Hunter, a Republican congressman from California, tried several times to introduce measures to offer an apology for slavery. Their measures got little traction in the US Congress though.

Some people argue that because slavery occurred more than a century ago, asking people to repent again is beating a dead horse. I understand that, but I also look around and see the legacy that slavery has left among black people—how it has damaged our sense of self-worth so severely and how other forms of bondage have risen up to take its place. We haven't fully exorcised this demon from our national soul. Until we do, our best strategy is to repent. When confession comes out of our mouths, sin is forgiven and room is made for love to come into our hearts. Through love, real change can happen. Creating laws to protect people's civil rights (and enforcing those laws) can bring about a degree of justice, but true justice will come only as we love one another and consider one another's needs as important as our own.

Let me clarify one thing here. I agree with those who object to blacks and other minorities who seek repentance from *only* whites. We have made progress, and it's not right to label ourselves victims or use racism (historical or present) as an excuse to do nothing. We shouldn't expect whites to solve our problems. What we can do is invite our white neighbors to join us in the efforts we are making to improve our lives and communities. The fact is that we were deprived for many years, but now we have opportunities—and we can sometimes still use a little help in order to fully take advantage of those opportunities. We don't want to use guilt to try to get people to help us; we want to use understanding about how God liberates us to enter into renewed relationships and move forward together. I need to be able to say to a white person I'm asking to help me with something, "This is not about you being wrong or me being wronged. This is about the time being right for us to work together in ways we never could before."

The damage that resulted from the old system of segregation has left African Americans in a hard state. The breakup of the family, laws and systems that have kept us from flourishing, redlining in housing developments, and so many other lasting effects of segregation make it so much easier for a black man to rob or hurt an innocent white person without much thought because of the damage that has been done. On the other side, the damage done to white people from centuries of racism makes it easier for them to avoid living in black neighborhoods, fear black people walking the streets, or even commit vicious hate crimes against blacks. The lasting guilt and lingering fears of racism cause people to view those who are different as being almost subhuman, rather than seeing them as children of God created in His image. This is why we talk past one another when racial incidents flare. This is why we ignore other people's stories or perspectives. This is why we always react defensively first, instead of humbly listening to and trying to understand the other side of the story.

But there is a better way. There is the way of Jesus Christ, shown to us on the cross—the most humble and grace-filled act there ever was. Due to our redemption, we have an obligation to forgive and accept the forgiveness of others. In forgiving and being forgiven, the healing process begins for both parties involved. Our acknowledgment of mistreatment and hurt is healthy for us; it's good for others too.

Right now we live in a country with a lot of fear and distrust and animosity between political parties, ethnicities, socioeconomic groups, generations, and other categories. And if we are being honest, our churches are just as divided by the same things. Maybe we will never have a perfect country or live in an ideal society, but the church must begin this process of confession and forgiveness. Can you imagine what it would be like to be a church that repents of systemic injustice and instead brings forth love and healing? What would it look like for us to love our neighbors across the aisle, our neighbors who watch a different news network, listen to different kinds of music, and attend different schools?

You have to be a bit of a dreamer to imagine a world where love trumps hate—but I don't think being a dreamer is all that bad. Joel prophesied that God would "pour out [His] Spirit on all people. Your sons and daughters will prophesy, your old men will dream dreams, your young men will see visions" (Joel 2:28). I'm an old man, and this is one of my dreams: that my descendants will one day live in a land where people are quick to confess their wrongdoing and forgive the wrongdoing of others and are eager to build something beautiful together.

12

Above the Noise

I consider myself to be first and foremost a Bible teacher. I'm an early riser, so Tuesday mornings I lead a Bible study with young leaders in my community, and we read the Bible and listen to God.

Listening to God and to one another is dreaming God's dream, and we are to live out what we hear. We are listening above the noise. Prayer is listening to hear God's voice. I was up early one morning (most mornings I am up before 4:30 a.m.) when I first came to know Jesus Christ. A friend had sent me to bookstore owner Mary Feester. She had been a missionary in Brazil, and we had become friends almost immediately. She had told me I needed to read through the Bible and see what was in it. Because I had received such little education at this point, I was timid about tackling such a giant task, but she assured me I could do it and guided me in doing so.

So one morning I was reading through the Bible as she had suggested when I came to the story of the call of Abraham. As I read, I realized that the blessing of Abraham was really for others. The blessing was to be a blessing. I heard the call of Abraham—the call that all the world would be blessed through him—and I heard that call on my own life. Bible teaching is hearing God speak in prayer, obeying it, and then trying to put it into practice. A Bible teacher has to listen. You have to listen to the people you are teaching, but even more important, you need to listen to God.

For me, praying really is more about listening than asking. When we do all the talking, we're not listening to God. We are not hearing His will, His plan, His desire, His pleasure. In prayer, we come to God with our needs, agony, and thanks. But too often people end their prayers right after making all of their requests.

When I pray I would much rather God do most of the talking, even if I don't get to express every need on my list. In the long run, if He hears our longings, do we have to spell out every specific detail? How can we be obedient if we never hear His instructions or the wisdom He has to offer? We want things to happen when we pray, so we have to let God do the talking and the Holy Spirit do the empowering.

When the prophet Elijah prayed, things happened. The widow of Zarephath's son was healed: "The LORD heard Elijah's cry, and the boy's life returned to him, and he lived" (1 Kings 17:22). The prophets of Baal were put to shame:

> At the time of sacrifice, the prophet Elijah stepped forward and prayed: "LORD, the God of Abraham, Isaac and Israel, let it be known today that you are God in Israel and that I am your servant and have done all these things at your command. Answer me, LORD, answer me, so these people will know that you, LORD, are God, and that you are turning their hearts back again."
>
> Then the fire of the LORD fell and burned up the sacrifice, the wood, the stones and the soil, and also licked up the water in the trench. (1 Kings 18:36–38)

Weather patterns were changed: "Elijah . . . prayed earnestly that it would not rain, and it did not rain on the land for three and a half years. Again he prayed, and the heavens gave rain, and the earth produced its crops" (James 5:17–18). These were pretty dramatic answers to prayer, so it's not surprising that we tend to make a big deal out of this aspect of Elijah's communication with God. It can be easy to forget the other side of Elijah's prayer life—the listening side. But if we look at the Scripture passages, we see this pattern a lot: "Then the word of the LORD came to Elijah . . ." (1 Kings 17:2), followed by "So he did what the LORD had told him" (1 Kings 17:5). Elijah's life was a series of obedient steps—he heard from God, and then he acted on what he had heard. I believe this is a key truth about prayer: it's much more about listening to God than it is about telling Him things—information we think He should have, things we think He should do, or whatever else we might tell Him.

In fact, I believe Elijah would point to a listening moment if he had to choose his most profound prayer experience. At Mount Horeb—exhausted, discouraged, and afraid for his life—Elijah had a conversation with God. He told God some things—how hard his experience had been and what a difficult situation he was in now. In return, God gave him a lesson in listening. A great wind, an earthquake, and a fire came and went—now these were impressive signs of God's power, but the presence of the Lord wasn't in them. Then came a gentle whisper that Elijah recognized as the voice of God. Elijah stood there in God's presence, and again he told God some things—the same things he'd told Him before, as a matter of fact. But God had something else He wanted to discuss: what He wanted Elijah to do with the last part of his life. He told Elijah how he could finish well. My translation: "I want you to make a couple of kings, and then I want you to get yourself a successor. And then you're out of here so you can come home and be with me. You have fought the good fight, finished the course, welcome home" (see 1 Kings 19:15–16).

What did Elijah do in response to what God told him? "So Elijah went from there and found Elisha son of Shaphat. . . . [who] set out to follow Elijah and became his servant" (1 Kings 19:19, 21). Later, Elisha went to both of the men God had named and anointed them king (see 2 Kings 8 and 9).

I think most of us at least start out making prayer about us talking to God—and certainly, God invites us to do that. Paul instructs us, "In every situation, by prayer and petition, with thanksgiving, present your requests to God" (Phil. 4:6). The big question is will we, like Elijah, be willing to take the time and trouble to listen to God as well? Certainly, if God spoke dramatically—with a wind, an earthquake, or a fire—while we were praying, we would probably hear that. But do we listen carefully for the still, small voice of God when we pray? Once we hear it, are we willing to obey, even if what God says doesn't exactly address the concerns we brought to Him in the first place?

I have found myself coming to love more deeply the Lord's Prayer (see Matt. 6:9–13). Many Bible teachers and theologians use this prayer as a pattern, and I think that's a good way to look at it. After all, it was Jesus teaching His disciples to pray! But what I really love about the Lord's Prayer is what it makes a priority for Christians.

It starts by acknowledging the bigness, sovereignty, and power of God: "Our Father in heaven, hallowed be Your name" (Matt. 6:9 NKJV). It's like the angels that surround His throne, as we are told in Revelation 5:11–14 we will someday do, praising the greatness of our God. Then "Your kingdom come" (v. 10 NKJV)—that promised beautiful kingdom that will come only when God's will is done "on earth as it is in heaven" (v. 10 NKJV). Next we acknowledge the daily provision God always provides by asking, "Give us this day our daily bread" (v. 11 NKJV). And then, "Forgive us our debts, as we forgive our debtors" (v. 12 NKJV). As I said in the last chapter, forgiveness is powerful and necessary; it frees us from our sins and our burdensome relationships with others. "Do not lead us into temptation" (v. 13 NKJV), meaning keep us from sin before it even begins; lead us around it. "Deliver us from the evil one" (v. 13 NKJV), for when we do fall into temptation, we need deliverance from that evil. And we end with the blessed hope and glorious appearance of our Savior: "For Yours is the kingdom and the power and the glory forever" (v. 13 NKJV). The prayer puts the kingdom right there out in front of us. We are seeking the kingdom first, just as Jesus told us to, for when we seek the kingdom first, all the other things will be given to us as well (see Matt. 6:33).

Prayer led Shadrach, Meshach, and Abednego right into a fiery furnace. It led Daniel right into a lions' den. Prayer allows us to prioritize the kingdom and the will of God, not our own desires. Prayer is meant to change our list of desires so that we instead seek God's kingdom and the things He wants rather than the comforts and riches of this world.

Now, I'm not saying we should never pray for our children or sick family members or bring our concerns to God. I believe He finds our prayers to be like fragrant offerings lifted up in the midst of pain and suffering (see Ps. 141:2, for example). In fact, healing and strong families are all in line with the picture God gives us of His flourishing kingdom. My point, though, is that the joys and petitions we offer to God will probably look a lot more like His will if we pray for His kingdom first.

I'm growing in my understanding—and practice—of prayer in my old age. The way I've come to define prayer is that it is seeking and listening for the voice of God in relationship to His will. This is my goal when I come to God in prayer. I've discovered that one way to listen to God is simply to take the time to think about a decision instead of making it right away. That has been hard for me, but I am learning not to be so hasty with my decisions. I make it a point now to reflect on opportunities that are before me and ask God, *Should I do this? Is this Your will? Is there another way that's better?* This is something I always want to be working on and growing in.

Earlier I referenced the passage of Scripture that describes how Paul had made up his mind to go to Bithynia, but the Spirit stopped him, and God ended up sending him and his missionary team to Macedonia instead (see Acts 16:6–10). Sometimes God intervenes like that in my life too—though I've yet to see a vision of a Macedonian man asking me for assistance. After Hurricane Katrina, I decided to buy a truck so that the John and Vera Mae Perkins Foundation could deliver donated materials and supplies to people who'd been devastated by the storm. I had the money and was getting ready to buy a used truck. The need was urgent, and I don't like to procrastinate. But I decided to wait for a short time, and I asked God for His guidance—for Him to show me if He had something else in mind. One day I was on a road I travel a lot, and there was a used truck for sale that looked like a perfect fit. Instead of spending $18,000 for a truck, I was able to buy the used one for $2,500, and it met the same need. Ten years later, that truck is still running without any mechanical failures. It's a perfectly good truck—it can haul a trailer, and it did everything I needed it to do while I was helping with Katrina's aftermath. I'm glad I didn't rush into the first opportunity that presented itself but instead gave God a chance to show me another way.

However, I do have to offer a word of caution. Prayer can be used as a delay tactic. We say, "Oh, I'll pray about that," because we don't want to commit to doing something. We want to wait on God, but we don't ever want to use prayer as an excuse for procrastinating. When considering what to do after Hurricane Katrina, it would have been easy to get stuck in a mental game of pros and cons: *The used truck costs less, but the other one would be more reliable, and God gave me enough money to get the more expensive one, but maybe He wants us to do something else with some of that money . . .* It could have gone on and on, and I could have said the whole time, "I'm praying about it and waiting for God to give me clear direction." That would have been procrastination, not intercession. That would have been using prayer as a reason for not meeting a need that God had equipped me to meet. So it's a challenge, and it really comes down to faith—believing that God has given you what you need to make a good decision and move forward with the work you're doing for Him. Prayer is not a substitute for action; it is a preparation for action.

When Elijah was at Mt. Horeb, prayer wasn't just about talking to God or even just about hearing from God—it was about experiencing God's presence. That has become another way that I think about prayer: it's the assurance that God is with me. It's the acknowledgment of His presence. It's the assurance that He hears me and guides me because He is not only up there or out there, but He's also in the room with me. When I get ready to do something for God—preach, for instance—I know God is with me. So it almost seems a little odd to pray at the beginning of my message, but I think it's good to acknowledge God's presence, so I do that. The prayers that feel more significant to me are the moments prior to my speaking. I try to be alone (often in a bathroom stall, since that's a good place to be alone!), listening to God and asking Him if there's something He wants me to say to this group of people that I haven't thought of. I also ask Him for wisdom about how to start each presentation. I've learned that if I don't get started in a way that connects with people, it's very hard to draw them in by the time I'm done. That's really what I'm trying to do when I speak—connect with people and share with them what God has shared with me—so I seek His leading for that.

Being alone to pray has a lot of value. It's not just before speaking engagements that I find the bathroom is a good place to pray. In the shower in the morning is one of the places where I'm most likely to hear something from God. In fact, mornings in general are good for me. Early mornings, before I've had anything to eat, are when I feel most open, able to listen, and most creative—most likely to hear something I might not be expecting. Throughout my life, many of the times that I've heard from God—through His Word, through meditation, and through listening to Him in prayer—have been early in the morning.

Scripture gives us many examples of solitary prayer. Besides Elijah at Mt. Horeb, we read about Jesus going up into the mountains to pray, including on the night before He named His twelve disciples (see Luke 6:12–16); Jesus agonizing in prayer at Gethsemane while

His disciples slept a short distance away (see Mark 14:32–42); Paul hearing from the Lord in his cabin in the middle of the night that he and the other passengers and crew would not be killed in the coming shipwreck (see Acts 27:21–26); and others. The Bible also provides instruction on the matter of solitary prayer in the verses before the Lord's Prayer; Jesus said, "When you pray, go into a room alone and close the door. Pray to your Father in private" (Matt. 6:6 CEV).

One of the most important elements in our prayer is that we believe that what we are asking God for is in His will, because through prayer we remember God's promise, His covenant with His people, as we await the complete fulfillment of His will.

—✖—

Of course, corporate prayer is important too. Members of the early church devoted themselves to praying together, often with dramatic results. For example, "After they prayed, the place where they were meeting was shaken. And they were all filled with the Holy Spirit and spoke the word of God boldly" (Acts 4:31). The thing about our public prayer today is that it seems to be hard for us to listen to God in this context. We want to make corporate prayer a formula or part of a program—we offer a few words of praise, make some requests, and move on to the next item on our agenda. Many times, it even seems like our public prayers are simply holy sounding words said for the ears of the people in the crowd or service and not really directed toward God. We have work to do in learning how to pray together in such a way that we make room to hear God and respond to Him.

Corporate prayer is united around a purpose—a bigger issue. In Acts 12, the early church prayed for Peter while he was in jail, and miraculously, he was set free. It was a group of people coming together to pray for a big purpose. Corporate prayer is when we should pray for the big issues that prevent the gospel from going forward—the killings, the racism, the hatred, the crime. It is the 2 Chronicles 7:14

type of prayer, where God calls His people to humble themselves and call on His name, so that He will heal their land. That should be our picture of corporate prayer.

While I believe that listening to God is the most essential element of prayer, I see prayer as having value for other reasons as well. For one thing, prayer is a powerful example as we witness. It says to those who see us praying that we know God and believe that He communicates with us. It demonstrates our dependence on God—our faith that this unseen God does in fact enter into the affairs of human beings.

Prayer—and in particular, God's response to prayer—can also deepen the faith of those who already know Him. Dixie Noble is passionate about prayer. Dixie and her husband, Lowell, have spent eight or nine months a year, for more than fifteen years, living and working with our small staff at the foundation in Jackson. Dixie probably spends the majority of her time either praying or talking about prayer. She goes on prayer walks, she's in prayer groups and prayer partnerships, she makes sure we pray together as a staff at the foundation, she reads books about prayer—Dixie *loves* prayer. She also loves people; she grieves when people are hurting and cries out to God on their behalf.

A while back, Dixie entered a season of pain—physical pain. She'd had surgery on her hand, and there were complications that caused her terrible pain. I couldn't touch her hand without hurting her. She went to doctors and wore splints and did exercises—and these things helped some, which she was grateful for, but she was still in pain. Then one day a group of volunteers prayed over her hand—and the terrible pain went away. No, her hand wasn't quite back to normal, but it was much better. She could use it again. People could touch it without hurting her. I kind of think God put her through that experience to give her an opportunity to see the power of prayer in a tangible way. Her personal experience confirms the devotion she already had and motivates her to continue to pray, even when the results aren't immediately visible. It also speaks to those of us around her—we see that what she has been saying all along is right. Prayer matters. God does things in response to prayer.

—⟡—

In the early days of my ministry, I was called a storefront evangelist, which meant that I visited a lot of small churches. I wasn't well-known back then. I didn't have the kind of reputation that would get me an invitation to speak to the larger congregations, so I would go pretty much wherever they would have me.

A lot has happened since then, and God has provided me with opportunities I never could have imagined. A few years ago, *Christianity Today* magazine called me a prophet to the white church in America. I embrace that. I'm honored that God would give me a message about justice and reconciliation to deliver to white American Christians. I've hoped that title wouldn't make it seem like I've neglected my own people to minister to whites. I don't believe I've done that, but sometimes when you get attention for one thing, people think that's the only thing you're about. That's one reason I'm especially grateful for the honorary degree I received recently from Virginia University of Lynchburg, one of the oldest theological schools founded and continuously managed by blacks. I feel a certain amount of redemption there, and again, I'm grateful that God has given me words about forgiveness and responsibility to speak to my brothers and sisters in the black church. To be able to speak to Christians of all ethnicities in churches and universities across the country is an amazing privilege.

When I reflect on my life and all these years of ministry, I understand a little bit better what Jeremiah meant about the Lord saying, "Before I formed you in the womb I knew you, before you were born I set you apart; I appointed you as a prophet to the nations" (Jer. 1:5). That's not to compare myself to Jeremiah, but just to say that I have a similar feeling that God must have had some purpose for my life way back at the beginning. I still think often about my mother dying, and me living, and my sense that He must have had something He wanted to do in and through me. I look back at some of the crucial times in my life, and I see how God has revealed His redemptive grace in different ways at different times.

When I was a child, even though we didn't go to church much, we occasionally attended revival services at a Baptist church. In hindsight, I'm sure the preachers spoke about the love of God and redemption through Jesus Christ, but I didn't hear that part when I was young. One thing, however, made an impression on me even then, when I was not yet a Christian. I remember one time hearing a preacher talk about Jesus in the Garden of Gethsemane—about Christ's suffering and pain and death. I didn't know what Gethsemane was, but somehow that caught my attention and stuck with me. Later in life, when I heard about Gethsemane again, I remembered that sermon and started putting the pieces together. *Hmm . . . that's where Jesus suffered. That's where He sweated drops of blood. That's where He endured pain.* And just like that, the idea that Jesus entered into our pain started to take hold in me.

Then there was that Sunday morning at a Church of Christ (Holiness) USA in Pasadena, California, when I finally heard the message about God's love—and felt that redeeming love enter my own heart. When I responded to that love, I was like the man in the parable about the treasure hidden in a field (see Matt. 13:44), trading everything he owned for that field. I exchanged the chance for a peaceful and successful life for me and my family in California to return to the dangers, racism, and poverty in Mississippi. I had no way of knowing how much good God would bring out of that decision, but I was compelled to follow and obey this God who loved me.

I believe God has purposes for all of His people. And it's difficult to get around those purposes. As I look back, I see how God was at work to fulfill His purposes for me, even before I began to understand them. I tell people now to try to find that place in their life where they sense God is calling them to do something. Really, I think that's what conversion is. It's coming to the realization that God loves us, and then looking for how He wants us to hold that good news about Him up for the world to see. As we do that, the Holy Spirit takes our witness to the gospel and applies it to people's hearts.

Scripture contains many beautiful examples of people who were willing to give up what they had—or what they could have had—to participate in God's work in the world. When Zacchaeus encountered Jesus, he said, "Look, Lord! Here and now I give half of my possessions to the poor, and if I have cheated anybody out of anything, I will pay back four times the amount" (Luke 19:8). Following Jesus's death, Nicodemus provided expensive embalming materials (see John 19:38–40), and Joseph of Arimathea put Jesus in a tomb that he was probably preparing for himself and his family (see Matt. 27:57–60).

Let's also look at John the Baptist. He was filled with the Holy Spirit from his mother's womb and wanted to seek God all of his life, so he went out to the desert and spent most of his time there, meditating on God. Who knows how much a dynamic preacher like John could have accomplished and how much wealth he could have accumulated had he decided to work within the existing power structure. But John didn't tie himself to the lusts and the things of this world. He was not drawn astray by a desire for comfort or material things. He ate wild honey and bugs, and he wore clothing of leather and camel's hair, so he didn't need money to live on. Because he didn't have a dependence on money, he wasn't intimidated by the people in society who did have wealth and power. He could say to the Pharisees, tax collectors, and others who came to him for advice: "Anyone who has two shirts should share with the one who has none, and anyone who has food should do the same" (Luke 3:11).

In fact, most of John's warnings had to do with money—and the just handling of money. He told tax collectors not to collect more than they were due, and he told soldiers not to extort. He was able to shine a light on how the Pharisees had allowed their love of money to infect their religion. He showed himself as a prophet who understood God's justice and redemptive love for humanity.

—⁓—

Of course, we always have to be on the lookout for false prophets and teaching that leads us away from the truth of Scripture. Some are false prophets who sometimes don't offer a full teaching. Later, if you talk to such people, they'll say, "Oh, no, that's not what I meant." So they may have an accurate biblical understanding, but they are not responsible teachers of the Word. As Christians, we have the responsibility to be alert to both of these dangers and to ask our teachers questions.

We also need to ask God continually for wisdom. No doctrine or formula can replace wisdom and understanding. Our two greatest needs as human beings are to know Jesus and to be discipled in wisdom. Many people look to teachers for knowledge only, but wisdom is what we need—wisdom that we gain by listening to and for God as we make our way through life.

Recently I was in a theological discussion with a group of people. They asked me what I thought should be the church's next great venture. My answer was pretty simple: unstop our ears—take these earbuds out of our ears. There is too much noise in our society right now, and that noise just keeps getting louder. We need quiet time for reflection. We need to be still and know that God is God.

13

The Church of the Future

I love history and even consider myself to be a bit of an amateur historian. However, as Christians, there is a proper way to look at history. The book of Revelation describes God as the One who was and is and is to come. God is the same yesterday, today, and forever and does not find Himself trapped by time in the same sense that human beings do. So, while most people consider history to just be looking at the past, I think Christians should take a more holistic view of history, looking at it for what was, what is now, and what is to come and seeing all of these pieces connected as part of a plan set forth by an infinite and all-knowing God.

We reflect on the past to get a good picture of what has happened, what we have done well, and what mistakes we have made. In light of that information, we ask the question: How shall we live now? If all of the past discipleship and biblical teaching has any meaning, then it needs to influence how we are living today. But we also must look at where we are going. We know God holds the future in His hands, and His plans and purposes are working themselves out, but that does not mean Christians are just passive observers.

In the Old Testament, the prophets proclaimed God's plans and purposes to the people of Israel. But as I look at the end of the

Gospels, at the giving of the Great Commission, Jesus's ascension, and then the beginnings of the early church in Acts, it is clear that God has called His church to be the prophetic voice in our society today. Peter and James, in particular, write that God is calling out His church to be His people who bear His name and relay His will and purposes to the world (see 1 Pet. 4 and James 2).

If these called-out people are going to proclaim God's intentions and be faithful witnesses to the plan God has for our lives, then the people of the church have to live lives that mirror Jesus. The church must be salt and light in the world (see Matt. 5:13–16). We are redeemed and join with Jesus in His redemptive work. Of course, we must first admit that we are sinful and broken people, and it is God's grace and love for us, not our works, that save us. But when our individual lives and our communal life as a church are marked by these redemptive actions, that is pretty good evidence that we are being redeemed.

During my lifetime, I fear that more people have seen the church as a messy contradiction defined by division and hot-button issues than have seen it as a prophetic voice living out the gospel. Most people outside the church see it estranged regarding issues of race, economics, sexuality, and so many other things. They see the church as a place that condemns, rather than loves. They hear the voice of the church speaking a language of hate, rather than a language of redemption and reconciliation. We have lost the fullness of the gospel.

It's time to recover the fullness of the gospel, to embrace a more holistic approach to ministry. We need to recapture the richness of the incarnation, the idea that God came down in the person of Jesus Christ to save the whole person—body, soul, and spirit. He came to minister to people in their sick and miserable states as well as in their healthy and joyful states.

Many people, especially in the younger generations, have given up on the church—sometimes because of the segregation and hypocrisy they see there. My friend Shane Claiborne discovered this truth through some informal research:

> A friend and I prepared a video clip once for a worship service. Our goal was to capture other people's responses to the word Christian, so we took a video camera and hit the streets, from the trendy arts district to the suburbs. We asked people to say the first word that came to mind in response to each word we said: "snow," "eagles" (it's Philly), "teenagers," and finally "Christian." When people heard the word Christian, they stopped in their tracks. I will never forget their responses: "fake," "hypocrites," "church," "boring." One guy even said, "used-to-be-one" (sort of one word). I will also never forget what they didn't say. Not one of the people we asked that day said "love." No one said "grace." No one said "community."[1]

Shane goes on to write, "Over and over I see people rejecting God because of the mess they see in the church. . . . But I have tremendous hope that a new kind of Christianity is emerging."[2] He tells stories of some of the "extremists for love" he has met both at home in the United States and halfway around the world in places like Iraq and India. These stories give me hope. I am encouraged by Shane and his friends in Philadelphia and many other young people who are not yet willing to give up hope for what we can be as the church.

I want to see the church marked by something bigger than division, bigger than racism, bigotry, and hatred. The church has recently started talking a lot more about the Holy Spirit and the gifts of the Spirit. I hope that as we have these conversations, we will also start growing in the Spirit and bearing the fruit that comes along with that. Galatians 5:22–23 and 2 Peter 1:4–7 clearly lay out what this fruit is: love, joy, peace, forbearance, kindness, goodness, faithfulness, gentleness, self-control, knowledge, patience, perseverance, godliness, mutual affection, and love. What if these were the attributes of the church and the church's witness to the world? What a major difference this would make for all people on the earth!

—◊—

After World War II, many people had hope for a new vision in America. After seeing the atrocities committed by the Nazi Party and other fascist groups and what anti-Semitism did to Europe, we really should have been talking about the racial issues happening here—the segregation, the lynchings, the Ku Klux Klan, and the constant profiling. We also needed to remember the Native Americans removed from their homes in the Trail of Tears, the Japanese forced into internment camps, and all who were marginalized or oppressed due to their ethnicity or perceived differences. I think many people were hoping that America would enter a period of change and acceptance, but instead we started glorifying the homogenous. Maybe people thought it would create national unity after the war or something like that, but in the end, it did a lot more harm than good. Unfortunately, the church found itself swept up in this wave of homogeneity, and as we saw during the attempted pray-ins and church integrations during the civil rights movement, it stayed this way for a long time.

But starting in the 1970s, groups of us wanted to see something different happen. People like Ron Sider, Jim Wallis, Carl Henry, Paul Henry, Bill Pannell, my son-in-law Ron Potter, and the others who were starting Evangelicals for Social Action began meeting together. We started calling for more holistic development, for a new vision in the evangelical church. It was a long process, and we met a lot of resistance along the way, especially in the early days. But I think we are just now starting to see that vision turn into a new form of church growth. This is the first time in my life that I've witnessed extensive church planting, and not just in America, but all over the world. I am encouraged as I watch a new generation of leaders taking up this vision. For the first time, we are taking the idea of a cross-cultural church seriously, and we have a chance to see true reconciliation draw us together.

As I watch my work in ministry begin to come to a close, I can rest a little easier knowing that younger leaders are willing to continue the fight. I think of Tony Evans, the pastor at Oak Cliff Bible Fellowship in Dallas, Texas, and Mark DeYmaz, who started Mosaic Church in Little Rock, Arkansas, who are authentically modeling what a multiethnic church can look like. The KAINOS Movement, founded by Bryan Loritts, pastor at Abundant Life Christian Fellowship, and supported by pastors like Albert Tate from Fellowship Monrovia, is committed to seeing the evangelical church become more dedicated to diversity and social action. The Evangelical Covenant Church is a whole denomination that has focused its energy and resources into planting multiethnic churches. These are just a few examples.

When Jesus was here on earth, He talked constantly about the kingdom of God. The church is here to continue to witness to that kingdom, to remind the world of the promise Jesus made to come again and establish that kingdom in its fullness. But if we are to be faithful witnesses, then the church must start looking like the picture of that kingdom we see in Revelation. I have said this so many times, but it's worth repeating. The coming kingdom of God includes people of every ethnicity, of every generation, of every class. I'm glad Tony, Mark, Bryan, and so many others are modeling this in their churches, and I hope many other congregations take up the call to do the same.

—m—

I have watched us become a much more global society over the years, yet, in some ways, the world seems to have gotten a lot smaller. With the internet and other technology that allow us to connect, we can see one another, hear one another, and practically be with one another even if we're actually on opposite sides of the globe. We are meeting new people and hearing new voices, which has opened our eyes to the value of diversity in society. Our workplaces, schools, and perhaps now even the church—the place where true reconciliation can take place—have adopted a healthy appreciation and respect for diversity.

One influence our global sisters and brothers have had on American religious culture is the revival of house churches. In his book *Revolution*, George Barna notes that the house church is currently one of the fastest-growing models of church in the United States.[3] I believe this model of worship could be a really helpful approach for the future church in America. The first Bible lesson I ever taught was to a group of believers who met in someone's house, and I have always had a vision for small fellowship groups partnering with large churches. House churches make a lot of sense, especially in urban, and even suburban, neighborhoods.

During the first Great Migration from 1916–70, the time when many African Americans left the South and headed north in hopes of finding more opportunities and a better life, small storefront churches in the cities became the strength—almost the survival—of black communities. These churches often had pastors who worked other jobs, and they tended to be built around extended families. So much leadership and talent emerged out of these churches (particularly out of their music ministries) because in a small congregation, everyone has an opportunity to participate in worship life. These churches were vitally important because they were accessible to anyone in the community.

I visited and preached at a multiethnic church in Green Bay, Wisconsin, a few years back. After the service, the pastor was glowing as he told me that the ideas I'd shared in my message confirmed plans their congregation was already making. He told me how they were in the process of dividing up into home groups that could be vehicles for both discipleship of existing church members and evangelism to neighbors and friends. He wasn't kidding—that was exactly what I'd just been talking about! I had encouraged them to break the church down by zip codes and start seeing household groups as being the authentic church, and then invite community members into those fellowship groups. In those small groups, where people can get to know one another well and where they're already involved in each other's lives through being neighbors, the new converts can grow into fruitful disciples. Now I'm not saying the whole church can't still come together on Sunday morning, but that time becomes more of a jubilee—a time to sing and pray and celebrate the things God has been doing through the smaller fellowships during the week.

Over the past couple of decades, suburban megachurches have grown. I'm not necessarily opposed to these large congregations. In fact, I think they've done a good job of evangelizing and bringing people into the church. However, I do think that many of these congregations are in need of a better means of discipleship. Too often megachurches put their energy into entertaining people or meeting surface needs. I hear prosperity pastors promote only joy and happiness while missing out on real discipleship. James tells us to "consider it pure joy" when we face trials, for "the testing of your faith produces perseverance" and that perseverance will "finish its work so that you may be mature and complete, not lacking anything" (James 1:2–4). Joy out of tribulation is what will make us mature and faithful Christians, not just happiness for the sake of feeling good.

Many of these larger churches have started home groups and small groups, and I like some of that because it can be helpful in terms of discipleship. However, too often these groups end up being divided by money or class. People still like to stick together with those who are like them. In doing so, we again leave out the poor and disenfranchised in society.

Let me be clear, I am not just talking about more churches for the sake of churches. Churches have popped up all over my community that have taken over old, abandoned stores or buildings and tried to make them into churches. These churches might be in low-income communities, but too often they are just folks driving in from other areas who want a building to meet in. They are driven more by a pastor with a large personality who wants to start a church and do things their own way than by a concern about the hurting community around the church. These congregations focus a lot on singing and not a whole lot on hearing the Word of God or trying to be an incarnational presence of Christ in the neighborhood. These types of church plants are not what I'm talking about. These are not intentional communities seeking to reflect God's kingdom.

This brings me back to the idea of relocation. It is incredibly important for churches to be present in low-income communities. When churches are located solely in affluent suburbs, congregations often end up catering to the culture of the rich and either patronize the poor or forget about them altogether. A lot of these larger churches have an effective message and the ability to mobilize people well. I would like to see them using those attributes to aid in the planting of intentional, multiethnic, multiclass churches in low-income areas.

I repeatedly have seen this prove to be an effective model for church planting. During my time in Pasadena, I became good friends with Paul Cedar, the pastor of Lake Avenue Church, which became a partner in our ministry work in Pasadena. Both Bryan Loritts and Albert Tate, whom I mentioned earlier, were trained and equipped for ministry at Lake Avenue. Now both men have thriving, multiethnic congregations in areas of need. I hope Lake Avenue continues to train up new leaders.

Many churches in Memphis, Tennessee, have taken up the same model. Christ United Methodist Church, formerly pastored by Dr. Maxie Dunnam and now led by Dr. Shane Stanford, has been doing this type of work for years. Second Presbyterian Church, led by Sandy Wilson, and Hope Presbyterian Church, itself a church plant started by members of Second Presbyterian that grew into a large congregation, are also pioneering this effort in Memphis.

Bridgeway Community Church, a large congregation in Columbia, Maryland, is a multicultural church, pastored by Dr. David Anderson. But instead of just growing larger on their own, they too have begun to engage in this mission of church planting in urban communities. I am greatly encouraged to see so many of these large churches start to care more about the mission of the church than about their own personal gain.

Tim Keller is a friend of mine who perhaps has done this better than anyone else in recent years. Not only did he plant Redeemer Presbyterian Church in Manhattan, which has grown to more than five thousand members, but he also understands the need for and usefulness of church planting. He is now the chairman of Redeemer City to City, an organization that has helped start more than 250 churches in the United States and around the world. Many of these churches are located in the areas that need incarnational church ministry the most.

I don't have a magic number or formula, but I do think that once churches reach a certain size, it makes sense for them to be intentional in planting multicultural churches, sending out members as the base for these new congregations. Christian community, when it is meaningful and authentic, has a true redemptive element that is able to meet people's deepest needs. When we meet in smaller groups, we start to empathize with people more, to make their needs our own. We begin to love more fully and want the same things for the other members of our community that we want for our own lives and our own families.

When we start to care for others in this way, we find our lives quickly become intertwined. Our care for the poor stops looking like a handout and starts looking like the way we care for family members and those we love. We start trying to find ways to get people jobs, to get people good educations, and to provide opportunities that they might not otherwise have. We start getting more creative in the way we approach mission.

Perhaps the best example of this that I have ever seen is the one set forth by my best friend, Wayne Gordon, at Lawndale Community Church in Chicago, Illinois. Wayne, or Coach as most people know him, moved to North Lawndale in 1975 to coach and teach at a local high school.

As Coach began to lead a Bible study with some of the high school boys through Fellowship of Christian Athletes, he and his wife, Anne, and the boys began to talk about starting a church. But Coach and Anne didn't want their church to simply be a place that met people's spiritual longings. They lived in North Lawndale, one of the poorest neighborhoods in Chicago, so they knew the people's needs and wanted their church to be a community that takes care of the whole person—body, mind, and soul. And that's just what they've done. Community residents, mostly from Lawndale Community Church, founded the Lawndale Christian Health Center, a facility that sees more than 150,000 people each year, and the Lawndale Community Development Corporation, which helps with educational needs, economic development, and housing ministries. This is not to mention the hundreds of people Coach has discipled and developed into leaders who are now joining in the work of ministry and seeking ways to uplift their community.

Coach is amazingly gifted at mobilizing other congregations in the Chicago area to join with the people of Lawndale Community Church to work together to bring more holistic change. I long for the day when churches like Lawndale and pastors like Coach become the norm, rather than the exception to the rule.

—⚏—

Part of the reason the church in America faces some of its current challenges is because of where we live and how we see the gospel message. The fullness and adequacy of the gospel is a message of togetherness and love across ethnic barriers. Churches that understand the fullness of the gospel and the greatness of God will serve people best. It's also important to understand that our problems are always multifaceted. Areas such as economics, behavior, family, and customs all stop us at the door to truth, when in reality, we should view these in light of God's justice.

We need to create an environment where truth can be told. Of course, we need the Holy Spirit to guide us in this task, but I think that can happen. This is really what our worship should be all about—seeking and telling the truth. Ideally, both the preacher and the congregation are there for this purpose. They should hope to hear and discover truths about themselves, about society, and about doing life together. And then, in the midst of seeking and telling truth, we find God's presence.

This is perhaps the strongest form of community, a group of people who tell one another the truth. When we're honest with one another about our lives, our struggles, and what we are doing, we grow to be a family. We find ourselves spending time together after church. We don't only sing praise songs together in the sanctuary; we actually live out our lives together. We find ourselves refreshed in the presence of others. We sit together in our yards and enjoy our children and grandchildren. This type of community among believers makes me think of Zechariah 8:4–5, which says, "Old men and old women shall again sit in the streets of Jerusalem, each one with his staff in his hand because of great age. The streets of the city shall be full of boys and girls playing in its streets" (NKJV). Maybe it's because I'm a great-grandfather that I find this idea particularly refreshing, but isn't it beautiful to imagine people from every walk of life spending time and doing life together?

People often look back and idealize the community of the early church. While we need to be careful not to paint an overly romantic picture of what went on during that time, I think we can learn a lot from their communal life together. Acts 2:44 says that believers held everything in common. Everything. They supported one another and looked after people's needs, making sure that every community member was cared for.

But not only that, they were also adding to their number daily. They were out evangelizing, discipling, and enfolding new people into their community. They also lived with a sense of urgency. They thought Jesus would be coming back any day, and they lived like it. They didn't put off the task of being the church and community they were called to be until the next day, because they didn't know if the next day would ever come.

The church today has lost that sense of urgency. We have slipped into a complacency that often causes us to put off for tomorrow the tasks that should be done today. Paul told us to be watchful, to be on our guard. He said when Jesus comes back, it will be like a thief coming in the night. If we truly believed we were living in the last days, our churches would look much different; they would look a lot more like the one we read about in the book of Acts.

—◊◊◊—

If I am being completely honest, I am not overly enthusiastic about the church right now. I have seen a lot of things go wrong and have found myself disappointed by the church more times than I care to remember. But despite my disappointment, I am hopeful. I am hopeful that many of the ideas I have shared in this chapter, and throughout this book for that matter, will start to take root and grow. I hope for the church in Revelation that I am so desperately longing for.

I hope the church in America will snap out of its complacency and be a witness to this nation—and the nations of the world. Sometimes I fear that this is just a pipe dream. I fear that we have missed our opportunity to be the prophetic voice we were called to be. These days I often find myself quoting 2 Chronicles 7:14, which says, "If My people who are called by My name will humble themselves, and pray and seek My face, and turn from their wicked ways, then I will hear from heaven, and will forgive their sin and heal their land" (NKJV).

My hope and my dream is that the recent events in cities like Ferguson, Missouri; Baton Rouge, Louisiana; and Dallas, Texas, and the subsequent stories of violence and the devaluing of human life will spur people on toward change. I'm hoping that as the church ponders the crisis in the Middle East and all that groups like ISIS are doing, they will offer an alternative—a better response that draws people into the deep love of Christ, rather than the hands of hatred and killing. I'm hoping the church will remember that our repentance still hasn't been deep enough. I am hoping we will wake up and start confessing our sins, learning to be humble before God. Perhaps the great joy that comes with redemption and the promise that Jesus Christ has defeated death will give us the energy and courage to do just that.

Think about it. If we actually went to church together, if we actually considered our brothers and sisters of different ethnicities and classes to be vital members of the body of Christ, what a great witness we would be for the world in which we live! I am all for churches being a part of the nonviolent marches and protests that have happened in the wake of violent killings, but these protests happen only after a tragic event has taken place.

I want the church to be what prevents these acts from ever happening. I want the church to be the community that is so dedicated to loving our neighbors, to caring for the poor and neglected, and to living out true reconciliation that these killings do not even take place. I want the white police officers to be sitting next to the young black boys in church on Sunday, singing songs and praying together, learning to be members of the same family of God. I want the single black mother and the family that recently emigrated from Latin America to go up and take Communion together. I want the older widow, who has been living out a lonely life in a nursing home, to be visited and cared for by the young man whose third-grade test scores said he would end up in prison someday. I want this to be the picture of the church. I want to see a *real* community of love.

Everyone wants to fight crime, fight violence, fight racism, and fight injustice, but love is still the final fight, and unless we have these communities of love, we will never see this dream realized.

14

Dream with Me

I started off this book claiming to be a dreamer. Throughout these chapters, I hope you have seen some of the dreams that I have had and continue to have today. Some of these dreams I have seen realized, while others I have not, but many I still hold on to today, hoping to eventually see them come to their full extent.

We live in a society that was built on dreams. America was a dream some people had for a place where *all people* could be seen as equals and have a voice, where all people were given certain rights. America has failed to make that happen, but I have watched people try to carry it on. Martin Luther King Jr. certainly tried, desiring a nation where his four children could be considered based on their character rather than on their skin color. He knew this dream was deeply rooted in the American dream itself—the real American dream, that is—of liberty and justice for all.

That dream is my dream too. I wish I could say that in my lifetime we achieved it, but we certainly haven't. I look specifically at my sons, my grandsons, and now my great-grandsons, recognizing that they have to grow up in fear, knowing that all too often, especially in our criminal justice system, our black boys are judged for the color of their skin and not the content of their character. I look at my neighborhood around me—our broken school systems and the neglected state of the poor—and I realize we are not there yet.

When I become too discouraged or am tempted to give up on this dream altogether, I am reminded of the prophet Isaiah's vision of this improbable future: "The wolf will live with the lamb, the leopard will lie down with the goat, the calf and the lion and the yearling together; and a little child will lead them" (Isa. 11:6). As a black person in Mississippi in the 1930s and '40s, and again in the '60s and '70s, I sure did feel like a lamb among wolves sometimes. Not that we black folks were purely innocent victims, of course, but we lived in a constant state of vulnerability, with a never-ending undercurrent of fear. Danger lurked around every corner, and so did opposition and discouragement. We expected that every door we approached would be not only closed but also locked. We knew we would have to fight and wait and fight some more to get through that door.

While our situation might not be quite as desperate today, I think a lot of my people are still finding closed doors, even if they're no longer locked. I remember what a huge role young people played in the civil rights movement of the 1960s and '70s, and I am so thankful for how far their efforts and commitment got us. I'm tremendously proud of my own children and our other Mendenhall young people, as well as students from nearby universities, who marched with us, integrated local facilities, and even went to jail with me. But if this dream of equality is to continue, we need the young people of today to take up that mantle and continue the fight for justice for all. As I travel across the country talking to young people, particularly at conferences and colleges, I am encouraged to see so many of them ready to take up this dream and do something about it.

It's natural to want to support people who are like us, and it's no surprise that we want them to do well—especially when some of those people are leading the way for minority groups who have historically been excluded from certain opportunities. When Barack

Obama was elected president of the United States in 2008, it meant something to blacks. When Kristi Yamaguchi won a gold medal in figure skating at the 1992 Olympics, it meant something to Asian Americans. And when Louis Brandeis was named the first Jewish US Supreme Court justice back in 1916, it meant something to Jewish people. And that's good! It's important to recognize these events. There's nothing wrong with celebrating the achievements and progress of members of our own race or ethnicity.

It's just that we can't stop there. The Bible has a greater commission for those of us who believe in Jesus Christ. We are to want not just good things but the best thing—salvation—for all. Jesus instructed His disciples to go into the world and preach the gospel to every ethnic group. God's good news is for everyone—everywhere on the earth. Many of us, because we have grown up in a segregated society, experience fear, discomfort, and even pain when we think about venturing across so-called racial lines to develop relationships and do good for one another. But if we're not doing this, are we really fulfilling the Great Commission? Are we really being the church?

When I look at the book of Acts in particular, I see an undiscriminating attitude clearly displayed. Look at Phillip and his willingness to sit and explain the Scriptures to the Ethiopian. Look at Paul and his desire to go to every nation and preach the gospel. These are the models we have been given. These are the types of ministries we should be emulating.

—⁓—

I think we are in need of a new language. For too long we have been constricted by a language of hate, always speaking negatively and finding ways to put people down. We need a new language—one of love—that affirms and heals, instead of wounds and destroys. I have met some people who are also looking for this language of love. They believe the church can and should be a more loving, reconciled, and grace-filled environment, and they are making their voices heard in Christian circles. I have seen them at our CCDA conferences, at an immigration rally in Phoenix, and at places like Urbana or the Justice Conference.

They're going to change more than just the conversation though. These young people are ready to act. I remember so vividly the moment at the 2009 Urbana conference when a young man stood up and said, "Okay, we've had our conversations and our dialogue. When do we get to do something?" In that moment, I realized that I don't have to convince this generation that racism is wrong—that injustice and hatred are wrong. They're already convinced, and they're ready to do something about it. When I talk with these young men and women, we spend our time and energy considering how to create a new "beloved community" to replace the old segregated society we've lived in for so long.

I treasure several partnerships that provide me with ongoing opportunities to interact with young people who exemplify these values and characteristics. One is with Ontario Christian Schools (OCS) in Ontario, California. I met OCS's former superintendent, Leonard Stob, when I was invited to New Mexico to speak to the American Association of Christian Schools. In Leonard, I found a friend who was longing to communicate justice to this new emerging generation. OCS, in part because of its location, has a large percentage of Hispanic and multiracial students, and that contributed to Leonard's desire to develop a curriculum with justice at its center. He invited me to speak at both the high school and the elementary school. When I got there, I discovered that he and his faculty had done a wonderful job preparing the students for my visit. It was a joy to speak to these young people who received me so enthusiastically and kindly.

At OCS, I have met many young people who are excited about continuing the fight for love and justice. Leonard got me into some of the local churches to speak, and he also brought me back for one of their commencement programs, the school's biggest event. This community really wanted to hear my message about justice and love—the staff wanted it, the students wanted it, and the parents wanted it. But they didn't just want to hear it; they wanted to do something about it. So the school began sending groups, as part of a class, to work with us in Jackson. Working with these kids (and the adults in their lives) helps me to rest easy, knowing that the ministry of reconciliation that has been so important to me will continue with them.

We have also partnered with slightly older students at Seattle Pacific University (SPU) in Washington. This partnership began with a group of students who came to volunteer with us at the foundation several years in a row. Seattle is a multicultural city and, in some ways, seems to be a few steps ahead of other parts of the country in regard to overcoming prejudice and racism. The volunteers weren't particularly concerned about race, but they saw our indigenous leadership development efforts and the community work we were doing and helped accordingly.

One young woman in the group, Ruth, genuinely caught our vision. Ruth is energetic and passionate and after volunteering, she returned to campus, went to university president Philip W. Eaton, and demanded that he come to Jackson to hear what she and the other students had heard. He agreed to come and brought with him Tali Hairston, the then assistant director of campus ministries. Philip, who is white, and Tali, who is black, came up with the idea for establishing the John Perkins Center for Reconciliation, Leadership Training, and Community Development at SPU. Tali now runs the center, which has made an outstanding commitment to train and expose the whole student body—particularly those who will be entering other cultures—to reconciliation. I continue to maintain a close relationship with SPU and am excited to see where many of the students, trained by the center, will end up in the years to come.

—⁓—

Now I haven't deceived myself into thinking that these young people I've been describing represent the majority of America—or even the majority of their generation. I know that's not the case. In fact, I think recent events in our country, particularly surrounding police brutality in black communities, have shown us that we are far from being a completely unbiased society.

However, I believe I'm seeing what represents a significant movement within the Christian community, and I'm optimistic. People have gotten used to thinking in political terms, where it takes 51 percent to get something done. In social movements, however, it takes maybe 4 or 5 percent of the people to start bringing about change. So even if the people I'm talking about represent only a small percentage of the population, they still have great potential in terms of changing the landscape of the church so that we can be witnesses to our fellow citizens and America can reclaim its original promise to be a nation of liberty and justice for all.

The title of my first book is *Let Justice Roll Down*. I believe justice is what God wants—and what He is bringing to pass. Justice is a process, and change takes time, but I believe we ought to dream big dreams and make big statements as we pursue those dreams. Amos didn't tell the people that God wants justice to trickle through their society. The New Living Translation uses the phrase "mighty flood of justice" (Amos 5:24) to describe what God wants to see. One thing we learned in Mendenhall is that once flood waters start rushing through a place, there's no turning them back with human strength.

I visited South Africa a year before Nelson Mandela was released from prison and spent some time with members of his political party, the African National Congress (ANC). The ANC was still supposed to be outlawed at that time (technically, they were outlawed, but they were still prevalent), and their leader was in jail. But when I asked them if Mandela was going to be president of South Africa, they answered as if it had already happened. They were certain he would come out of prison, there would be an election, and the ANC would be in power—and they were right. Mandela's road to the presidency was far from easy, as it included twenty-eight years in prison. And the work in South Africa is ongoing. But when the wheels of justice start turning, the momentum is very hard to stop.

I believe we're experiencing some of that same momentum here in America. In large part, we've come to equate the phrase "American Dream" with big suburban homes and nice cars, but, as I mentioned earlier, the original American Dream was one nation, under God, with liberty and justice for all. The young, energized Christians I've mentioned could be the ones who make the American Dream, the dream as stated by Martin Luther King Jr., come true, but only if some courageous leaders are willing to step forward and risk their lives to make it a reality. At this moment, trying to be a fervent Christian might be the most patriotic thing a person can do, but only if it is leading us closer to this beautiful dream. For more than two hundred years we've reneged in so many ways on the words we've claimed are the foundation of our country. Now maybe, just maybe, we're about to see them come true.

When I talk about justice, I should be clear. I am talking about something much bigger and more beautiful than people getting what they deserve or an uncorrupt judicial system. As I mentioned earlier, I've come to understand that justice is an act of reconciliation that restores any part of God's creation to its original intent, purpose, or image. Justice is making right any of the many things that have gone wrong in this very good world that God made—and among the very good human beings He created to inhabit it. The first step in getting there is simply finding a new way to effectively talk to one another. Right now we are talking past one another. People are grouping up with those who look, think, and act like them, and then those groups are yelling past one another, refusing to listen. We have come to believe that there are so many differences between us that we cannot even communicate. We seem only to speak a language of hate.

But once we learn to talk to one another, we can start moving on to something bigger. We can move toward repentance and forgiveness. Right now, our forgiveness is too light. We speak the words, but they don't have any real weight. Real repentance and forgiveness requires psychological pain. It requires us to actually wrestle with what happened, to feel true remorse. Only when we are willing to grapple with the deep guilt and reality of our sin can we fully free one another with true forgiveness. The price is hefty, but the reward at the end is worth it.

Let's look at Adam and Eve, for example. When they were in the garden of Eden, God told them from the very beginning that if they ate the fruit of the Tree of the Knowledge of Good and Evil, they would surely die. But when Satan came into the picture, he convinced them to doubt God, and that bit of doubt was just tempting enough that Eve had to go and find out for herself what would happen. This is when sin entered the world. Sin enters when we doubt or stop trusting God, when we refuse to take Him at His word and instead go our own way. We create our own epidemics of sin, plunging the world into crisis, because we refuse to trust in the God who created everything good.

The truth is, human beings were created as one race—in the image of God. For some reason or another, though, we have doubted that central truth. We have allowed ourselves to believe we are divided by deep and irreconcilable differences, but that is not the truth of the gospel. When Jesus came and died on the cross to reconcile the world to Himself, He, through His blood, brought peace into this world (see Col. 1:20). But we have not allowed this peace to take root or these broken-down walls to be realized. Instead, we have tried to come up with human solutions and means of reconciliation. Instead of trusting in our great God, who created only one race and did the work of reconciliation for us, we have persisted in searching for ways to bridge a gap that doesn't even really exist.

The things that divide us are differences of ethnicity, nationality, and culture. Many of our differences result from the location and environment we were raised in or the various ways we were told to think or act. Maybe we imitated the behaviors of those around us. This does not mean one way a person was raised is right, while the others are wrong; it just means there are differences. More often, the most dangerous divide between us is our lust for power and deep greed that makes us hate our neighbors and think only of ourselves. But when we view ourselves as one race, one human race, I think we start to recognize that these differences are not insurmountable. We have a common place to start from. We must start viewing other people as human beings, not as obstacles to getting what we want. We can start believing that as members of the family of God, reconciled to Him through the blood of Jesus Christ, we are actually brothers and sisters.

The gospel's very purpose is to reconcile. The church is energized by a wholeness—by taking the gospel to the whole world. I think I have made that clear repeatedly throughout this book. But still, we have not come to fully understand this. "From one blood," we are told, God made "every nation of men to dwell on all the face of the earth" (Acts 17:26 NKJV). We have to start seeing this cohesion, this oneness. Right before Jesus went to the cross, He prayed that all believers, past, present, and future "may be one, as You, Father, are in Me, and I in You; that they also may be one in Us, that the world may believe that You sent Me" (John 17:21 NKJV). This was Jesus's prayer for us all, yet more often than not, I fear we have not lived up to it. Instead we fight for our own way, for our selfish desires, for our right to be superior. We build churches centered on our own cultural ideas of God, rather than on seeking to bring us back to Him. And then we fight with other churches and religions about who is serving their personal culture god the best.

Come dream with me. Dream of a fight for something bigger, something more important and worthwhile. We need to fight for justice and peace, for the walls between us to come crashing down. "There is one body and one Spirit, just as you were called to one hope when you were called; one Lord, one faith, one baptism; one God and Father of all, who is over all and through all and in all" (Eph. 4:4–6).

"Jesus Loves the Little Children," an old, popular children's song tells a simple truth that has not yet been realized. Vera Mae adapted the song a little to make it more fitting for the children who sing it at the John and Vera Mae Perkins Center for Reconciliation, Justice, and Christian Community Development:

Jesus loves the little children
All the children of the world
Red, brown, yellow, black, and white
They are precious in His sight
Jesus loves the little children of the world

Jesus's love is our model for love. If we truly love all people, we "shine among them like stars in the sky" (Phil. 2:15), pointing others to Christ. That's a dream worth the fight!

Gratitude

The greatest gift from God in my life has been, of course, His gift of grace and salvation. Close behind that is the gift He gave me in my wife, Vera Mae, and my family, including my eight children: Spencer, Joanie, Phillip, Derek, Deborah, Wayne, Priscilla, and Elizabeth. I am deeply grateful for the blessing my family has been in my life.

I am also deeply grateful for the support, advice, and friendship of those who have given so much of themselves to me. Friendship is a gift. That's grace—because it's undeserved favor. Loving God and loving friends are the essence of gratitude and redemption. In my eighty-six years of life, the deep friendships God has given me are precious. So, to all my friends, I am indebted and deeply grateful for your lives and your love. You found room in your hearts for me. What a blessing!

These committed people I call friends have sustained my life and ministry. That list starts with Mr. Wayne Leitch, the man who took this third-grade dropout under his wing, discipled me, and gave me the ability to believe that I could teach the Bible to others. It extends to Mama and Papa Wilson, who nurtured me even before I was converted and continued throughout my lifetime. The Wilsons had lost their only son in a car accident while I was in Pasadena, but Mama Wilson reached out to me and became the mother I never had, and

Papa Wilson gave me a father's love that my own father was not able to give. They embraced me.

Back in Mississippi, Archie Buckley and his wife, Fanny, embraced me and my family as their own children. Then there are the Mendenhall people, Dolphus and Rosie Weary, Artis and Carolyn Fletcher, and the early board of directors of Voice of Calvary Ministries: Lillian Fletcher, Robert Buckley, Jessie Newsome, Joe Paul Buckley, Martin Lott, Nellie Standfield, Dave Smith, Lillie Smith, Leonard Smith, Mitchell C. Hayes, Geneva Rubin, Hulon Ray Holmes, and Dr. Andrea Phillips. These people came around me from the start. These are the men and women who stood by my side in the sixties when the Ku Klux Klan was going to drive me out of town, after we had started our holistic ministry and were registering people to vote, as well as hosting civil rights meetings in our church and co-op store. They protected my life and showed me what it truly means to be willing to lay down one's life for a friend. They loved me first and wholeheartedly.

Many others came to be my friends over the years, including Jack McMillian, Dr. Kevin Lake, and Dr. Joel Heger. Any heroic act I might have done or any risk I ever took for the cause was due to their love and trust in me. Their love set a moral authority for me, so that I feared ever disappointing them. Proverbs tells us that the fear of the Lord is the beginning of wisdom, and I saw that reflected in the deep love these people had for me. I have had friends willing to give their lives, their money, their prayers, and their support on my behalf.

I have been blessed with friendship and commitment beyond what I ever could have imagined. Here is just a sampling of some of those people.

Jane Allen, Calvin Borne, Al and Marjorie Belton, Paul Cedar, Mark DeYmaz, Roland and Lila Hinz, Malcolm Street, George Moore, Jim Winston, James Howard, Dr. J. Vernon McGee, Wayne and Anne Gordon, Glen Kehrein, Mary Nelson, Bob Lupton, Ron

Spann, Herman Moten, Kathy Dudley, Elzar Pagan, Bob Penton, Jana Webb, David Evans, Bill Greig II, Norm Nason, Roy and Ruth Rogers, H. and Terry Spees, George Terzain, Howard and Roberta Ahmanson, Addie James, Al and Marion Whittaker, Dr. Gary Vander Ark.

In addition, I have to remember Steve and Stan Lazarian, Bill and Dinah Roberts, Bill and Susan Hoehn, Clevie and Carl Snell, Ken Smith, Dr. Philip Eaton, Tali Hairston, Victor Smith, Dr. Hudson T. Amerding, Dave Peacock, John McGill, Patricia Myers, Dr. Roger Parrott, Mr. Kurt Lamb and his family foundation, Margie and Cliff Michaelson, the Gundersen family, Vince Gordon, Ronnie Crudup Jr., Dan Wright and his whole family, Phil and Marcia Reed, Randy and Joan Nabors, Mr. and Mrs. Bill Magnum, Bishop Matthew Richardson, Dr. Will Norton Jr., Dr. Will Norton Sr., Johann Christoph Arnold and the Bruderhof Communities, Phil Yancey, Rufus Jones, and a host of other friends whom these pages do not allow me to list. Hundreds of you fit into this category.

I also must thank the institutions that have given me my honorary doctorates: Wheaton College, Huntington University, Gordon College, Geneva College, Spring Arbor University, Seattle Pacific University, Virginia University of Lynchburg, Belhaven University, Taylor University, Nyack College, North Park College, The Salvation Army College of Officer Training, and Whitworth University. Two institutions—The Salvation Army and Asbury University—bestowed on me the "Others" Award and the Foot and Basin Award, respectively.

To all these people listed, I owe my ministry, my successes, and my very life. I look forward to the day when we stand together in heaven and lay down any of the glory or fame we have achieved together at Jesus's feet.

Recommended Reading

For further information about the life and ministry of John Perkins, check out the following books.

Claiborne, Shane, and John M. Perkins. *Follow Me to Freedom: Leading and Following as an Ordinary Radical*. Ventura, CA: Regal Books, 2009.

God's Story for Me Bible Storybook: 104 Favorite Bible Stories for Children. Ventura, CA: Gospel Light, 2009.

Marsh, Charles. *The Beloved Community: How Faith Shapes Social Justice from the Civil Rights Movement to Today*. New York: Basic Books, 2005.

Nobel, Lowell. *From Oppression to Jubilee Justice*. Jackson, MS: Urban Verses, 2007.

Perkins, John M. *Beyond Charity: The Call to Christian Community Development*. Grand Rapids: Baker Books, 1993.

———. *Let Justice Roll Down*. Ventura, CA: Regal Books, 1976.

———. *A Quiet Revolution*. Waco, TX: Word Books, 1976.

———. *Restoring At-Risk Communities*. Grand Rapids: Baker Books, 1995.

———. *With Justice for All: A Strategy for Community Development.* Ventura, CA: Regal Books, 1982.

Perkins, John M., and Wayne Gordon. *Leadership Revolution: Developing the Vision and Practice of Freedom and Justice.* Ventura, CA: Regal, 2012.

———. *Making Neighborhoods Whole.* Downers Grove, IL: InterVarsity Press, 2013.

Perkins, John M., and Charles Marsh. *Welcoming Justice: God's Movement Toward Beloved Community.* Downers Grove, IL: InterVarsity Press, 2009.

Slade, Peter, Charles Marsh, and Peter Goodwin Heltzel, eds. *Mobilizing for the Common Good: The Lived Theology of John M. Perkins.* Jackson, MS: University Press of Mississippi, 2013.

Notes

Prologue

1. John M. Perkins, *Let Justice Roll Down* (Ventura, CA: Regal Books, 2006).
2. A. W. Tozer, *The Attributes of God: A Journey into the Father's Heart*, vol. 1 (Camp Hill, PA: WingSpread Publishers, 2003), 61.
3. Frederick Douglass, "The Meaning of July Fourth for the Negro," speech, Rochester, NY, July 5, 1852.

Chapter 1 Side by Side (but Not Together)

1. Hunter Bear, homepage, hunterbear.org/jackson.htm, last accessed June 22, 2016.
2. Ward Shaefer, "King Edward Re-opening Today," *Jackson Free Press*, December 16, 2009.
3. "Races in Jackson, MS (2013)," City-Data, accessed January 6, 2016, http://www.city-data.com/city/Jackson-Mississippi.html.
4. Martin Luther King Jr., "Letter from Birmingham Jail," April 16, 1963.

Chapter 2 That We Might Be One

1. Alex A. Alston Jr. and James L. Dickerson, *Devil's Sanctuary: An Eyewitness History of Mississippi Hate Crimes* (Chicago: Lawrence Hill Books, 2009), 193.
2. Fellowship Memphis Church, "Our Dream," accessed January 6, 2016, http://www.fellowshipmemphis.org/about-us/our-dream/.

Chapter 3 Poor Whites

1. Fannie Kemble, *Fanny Kemble's Journals*, ed. Catherine Clinton (Cambridge, MA: Harvard University Press, 2000), 62.

Chapter 4 Fighting without Fists

1. Martin Luther King Jr., "Address to the First Montgomery Improvement Association (MIA) Mass Meeting," speech, Montgomery, AL, December 5, 1955, available on Martin

Luther King Jr. and the Global Freedom Struggle, http://kingencyclopedia.stanford.edu/en
cyclopedia/documentsentry/the_addres_to_the_first_montgomery_improvement_association
_mia_mass_meeting.1.html.

Chapter 5 The Three Rs

1. Lao Tzu, "Quotable Quotes," Goodreads, accessed August 1, 2016, http://www.good
reads.com/quotes/215411-go-to-the-people-live-with-them-learn-from-them.

2. Oxfam, *Working for the Few: Political Capture and Economic Equality*, January 2014,
https://www.oxfam.org/sites/www.oxfam.org/files/bp-working-for-few-political-capture
-economic-inequality-200114-summ-en.pdf.

Chapter 9 Affirming Human Dignity

1. The phrase "Somebody's Daughter" was inspired by the song "Somebody's Daughter," John Mandeville and Steve Siler, 2005, Lifestyle of Worship Music BMI / Silerland
Music ASCAP.

2. Cheryl Miller, *The Language of Shalom: 7 Keys to Practical Reconciliation* (Victoria,
TX: Quantum Circles Press, 2012), 61–69.

3. Fanny J. Crosby, "Blessed Assurance," Hymns Unto God, last accessed June 27, 2016,
http://www.hymnsuntogod.org/Hymns-PD/B-Hymns/Blessed-Assurance.html.

Chapter 10 The Final Fight

1. A. W. Tozer, "The Genesis of Our Christian Faith," in *A Disruptive Faith*, ed. James L.
Snyder (Ventura, CA: Gospel Light, 2011), 11–12.

2. "Killings at Jackson State University," African American Registry, accessed May 5,
2016, http://www.aaregistry.org/historic_events/view/killings-jackson-state-university.

3. The Barna Group, "Americans Say Serving the Needy is Christianity's Biggest Contribution to Society," October 25, 2010, https://www.barna.org/barna-update/faith-spirituality
/440-americans-describe-christianity-contributions#.VytYwoQrKUk.

4. Ibid.

Chapter 11 The Power of Forgiveness

1. Corrie ten Boom with Elizabeth and John Sherrill, *The Hiding Place* (Grand Rapids:
Chosen Books, 2006), 221.

2. William Winter, speech, John Perkins Anniversary Celebration, Jackson, MS, June 2010.

3. King, "Letter from Birmingham Jail."

Chapter 13 The Church of the Future

1. Shane Claiborne, *The Irresistible Revolution* (Grand Rapids: Zondervan, 2006), 269–70.
2. Ibid., 270.
3. George Barna, *Revolution* (Carol Stream, IL: Tyndale House Publishers, 2005), 65.

John M. Perkins is cofounder of the Christian Community Development Association and director of the John and Vera Mae Perkins Foundation for Reconciliation, Justice, and Christian Community Development in Jackson, Mississippi. He is the author of many books, including *Let Justice Roll Down*, which was named by *Christianity Today* as one of the top fifty books that have shaped evangelicals.

WHEN **JUSTICE** AND **RECONCILIATION** MEET

The story of John Perkins is a gripping portrayal of what happens when faith thrusts a person into the midst of a struggle against racism, oppression, and injustice. It is about the costs of discipleship—the jailings, the floggings, the despair, the sacrifice.

And it is about the transforming work of faith that allowed John to respond to such overwhelming indignities with miraculous compassion, vision, and hope.

BE A PART OF THE
SOLUTION

The belief that all lives matter is at the heart of our founding documents—but we must admit that this conviction has never truly reflected reality in America. Movements such as Black Lives Matter have arisen in response to recent displays of violence and mistreatment, and some of us defensively answer back, "All lives matter." But do they? Really? This book is an exploration of that question. We cannot do everything. But we can each do something.

ALSO BY
JOHN M. PERKINS

LEARN MORE ABOUT
JOHN M. PERKINS
AND HIS WORK

Check out the John & Vera Mae Perkins Foundation website at

JVMPF.ORG

@JohnMPerkins   John&VeraMaePerkinsFoundation

John & Vera Mae Perkins Foundation
PO Box 10773
Jackson, MS 39289
601-238-4090
priscillaperkins81@gmail.com

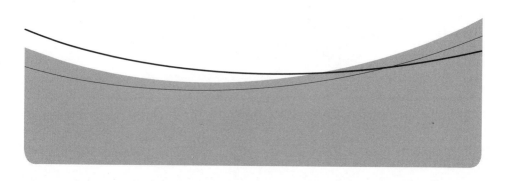